"Natasa is a woman on a mission. Driven, dynamic and empowered to deliver first class quality material."

– Lee Squire
Owner of Fernwood, Ballarat and Author of 'Death Debt & Drunk'
(Ultimate 48 Hour Author Retreat Attendee April 2014)

"I cannot use words high enough to explain what an inspirational person Natasa is. Through her program, I achieved to write and publish the book of my dreams."

– Sonia Scomazzon
Author of 'What Parents Repress Children Express'
(Ultimate 48 Hour Author Retreat Attendee October 2013)

"Natasa has developed a first class program in Ultimate 48 Hour Author. She is passionate about helping those who always wanted to write a book by showing them how easy it is."

– Laurence Sergovich
Author of 'The Mission'
(Ultimate 48 Hour Author Retreat Attendee July 2014)

"If you're looking for results in a supportive, professional, and fun environment, then U48A experience is for you."

– John Sharkey
Author of 'Quest to Freedom'
(Ultimate 48 Hour Author Retreat Attendee October 2013)

"I have exceeded my expectations in completing my whole book over the weekend. It's been absolutely amazing."

– Melonie Taylor
Author of 'Success on Purpose'
(Ultimate 48 Hour Author Retreat Attendee July 2014)

"Having coached many businesses and entrepreneurs, it is easy to see when an awesome rock star shows up to be coached. I've had such privilege in coaching Natasa personally. Her willingness to play full out, passion for her business and clients, an attitude of never settling for anything less than best is truly inspirational. Her life journey and honest attitude is an open book I believe every business owner should borrow a page from."

– Mihir Thaker
Business & Executive Coach (Natasa's Mentor)

"Natasa is a vibrant, brilliant and successful business woman, who not only 'walks her talk' but is also a fun and wonderful person to have around. She was always 'on call' for advice or that invaluable 'pep talk' whenever I needed her, plus she totally 'got me' and my business needs, and always provided a safe space for sharing personal challenges.

As a big vision thinker who is constantly dreaming up the next 'big project' with a gazillion creative ideas, Natasa was able to help me break it all down and focus on what was relevant now, as well as the next strategies required to propel my business. Natasa is the perfect blend of energetic enthusiast, fire-blazing action-taker and loving truth-teller. Align with Natasa and you'll experience fabulous new heights."

– Kym Mulcahy
Marketing Consultant (Natasa's One on One Mentoring Client)

"Having coaching support and training from Ultimate Weight Loss has made all the difference. I am now able to present myself with more confidence knowing that I have great products and a perfect system. I got my first paying client within two weeks of joining and have paid off my licensing fees within the first month of joining."

– Alana Carpenter
Living Slim Coach (Ultimate Weight Loss Coach Licensee)

Natasa DENMAN REVEALS...

1000 Days to a Million Dollar Coaching Business from Home

NATASA DENMAN

First published by Busybird Publishing 2015

Copyright © 2015 Natasa Denman

ISBN 978-1-925260-11-3

Cover image: Kev Howlett

Layout and typesetting: Jason Farrugia

Cover layout and design: Jason Farrugia

Busybird Publishing
PO Box 855
Eltham Victoria
Australia 3095

To my three generations of support that I learn from each and every single day. My mother, Ljupce, for giving me the opportunity to live in Australia and raising me to be independent, resilient and persistent. My husband, Stuart, for being the perfect opposite to support me in areas where I lack strength and talent and my three super awesome and gorgeous children, Judd, Mika and Xara, who inspire me to be the best person I can be as a parent, mentor and role model.

Contents

Introduction

I'm so excited that you've picked up this book and invested the time and the resources to learn how to grow your own million-dollar coaching business from home. The original idea of this book came to me about a year ago. I really wanted to write a book, more so for my children and personal reasons. I wanted to share with them how I grew up, the people that I was surrounded by and how certain beliefs have aided me or put blocks in front of me in life. I wanted to make it about the more vulnerable side of Natasa Denman. As the year progressed I got quite busy. 2014 was our million-dollar year in our business. I decided to put it on the backburner and about 6–8 weeks ago as I was sitting in a cinema watching *Rio 2* with the kids, the title of this book –*1000 Days to a Million-Dollar Coaching Business From Home* came to me and I thought why don't I kill two birds with one stone.

I decided to pull together both aspects of who I am – the personal and the business side – and put it out there for the public as well as my family and divide it into two parts. I'm always all about leverage and thinking of ways how it will assist me in my personal life and the legacy that I leave behind for generations, but also how it will aid other people in having the resources in the system that I have undertaken to get to where I am today.

So I decided seven days ago to start writing this book. As I record this introduction on a dictaphone – as it's how I write my books – I have already recorded every other chapter in this book, so this is the final piece of the puzzle.

Yet for you it's just the beginning.

I want to share how I grew up in Skopje, Macedonia where I lived until the age of 14. I want to share the challenges I've faced, the lessons I've learnt, the failures I've experienced and the resilience I've needed while transitioning from one country to another with a new language, new rules and a different culture. I want to share with you what really keeps me going: what my 'why' is, how I view the world and how I continue to discover my purpose. Each and every day my purpose becomes clearer and clearer as I evolve through the years as an entrepreneur, parent, mother, wife and daughter.

The first part of this book will be all about my personal story. In the second part I will explain the awesome business system that's going to enable you to build your own million-dollar coaching business from home.

I chose 1000 days because each and every day you must take consistent steps towards the outcomes you want to achieve. We're here to be present, we're here to make the most of each and every moment, to do the best we possibly can.

My first piece of priceless advice is: stop being a perfectionist! Perfectionism is looping and insane. I want you to go through this book embracing all the mistakes that you may come across and things that perhaps are not 100% perfect. I can guarantee you will find a few and my challenge to you is to be okay with them. If I worried about being perfect I would not have achieved what I have over the past 1000 days.

Doing something at 80% is better than doing nothing at 100%. Realistically if you can bring out what you want to help others at 80% or above, you're doing a great job, you're serving people, you're putting it out there. It's no good holding onto something for 5–10 years and then not being able to share your passion and message with others.

This book is mostly targeted for people in a services-based business. Individuals that are coaches, mentors, consultants, health and wellness practitioners and others who are selling their time and service. These are super-admirable professions, but at some point it does get tiring working with people one-on-one and we start to look for leverage to be able to enjoy the finer things in life and win back some of our time.

There is no magic bullet to building some serious leverage and it will most likely take you 1000 days to get there. I have chosen 1000 days because I don't want to be unrealistic, I don't want to make any false promises that something will happen in two months, because those kind of miracles are probably too far and few in between. They may have happened occasionally, however I believe business is a marathon and not a sprint. I also think that 1000 days is a very quick time to achieve what I have achieved. Out of those 1000 days, I was pregnant for 540 and had two children, including my son whom I had when I started the business. I've calculated that we've spent 270 days holidaying as a family, which is awesome. I've spent 45 days in live training where I have learnt and educated myself on how to build a business and be trained up as a coach and a mentor. I have been mentored one-on-one, 150 hours over that period. I have attended 500 networking events and coached over 2,000 hours one-on-one to become a certified professional coach through the International Coaching Federation.

I'm very proud to say that in 2014 I was a finalist in the Ausmumpreneur Awards for Product Innovation. For the last couple of years I was nominated for the Telstra Business Woman of the Year Awards. It was an honour to be nominated by some of my peers. All of these things have not happened overnight. There has been a build up to everything and a stepping-stone to the next growth and opportunity. One thing I want to make clear is that 9/10 things that you will try won't work. When you find what works for you, repeat, repeat and repeat them over and over again.

My mum always said this to me as I was growing up: *every beginning is hard*. It really stuck in my mind. She said it to me when I started school, when I moved to this new country, became a parent and when I started the business. I have this little figure in my mind that it takes a couple of years to really get through that hard part. I realised that that's how long it took me to settle into this country when I started my new jobs to master the skills with my previous career and as well when I became a parent. I adjusted to that a lot quicker, but my business, a couple of years was a time when I really had to focus and be truly uncomfortable to start getting real traction with my results.

So remember – every beginning is hard. I've changed it up a little bit when I'm teaching others, because I don't like the word 'hard'. Nowadays I say every beginning is awkward, or every beginning is unfamiliar. Take on my formula of two years, put your heart and soul into executing the actions you need to take to achieve success. Two years can fly by quickly if you're wasting time and are not focused. There's the famous saying that says – what you focus on is what you get to the exclusion of everything else. I had that ringing in my head for the first 6–12 months of business and it truly made me wonder if it's really true. Once I started seeing the results in my business I was certain it was true. Focusing mostly on my business growth it started to all come to fruition.

Another thing I've taken on board as a strategy is: *don't think, just act*. Put another way *is act before you feel*. It doesn't take me very long to make decisions. After reading a lot of personal development books myself, the most successful people have a strategy of making decisions fast, but changing them slowly.

You will find yourself and clarity through action.

Also be mindful of your creating versus consuming ratio. A lot of people love learning, reading books, attending seminars, going to retreats. They consume and consume some wonderful and valuable information. At the end of the day though, it's just information. To make it valuable for your life, you need to create your own information, your own knowledge and your own experiences. In writing this book, I've not referred to any manuals or books. I'm speaking from personal experience and except for a few notes I've written about some key points, everything is organic and natural. I will never teach anyone what I'm not willing to do or have not done myself.

Make your decisions fast, stick them out, because people quit way too soon and usually just as success is around the corner. Listen to your subconscious mind. Become an intuitive person, because oftentimes we get messages from our subconscious that guides our way to success.

An example of this is coming up with the title of this book. I asked my community and mentor for their opinions. Many people said it should be 3 years or 36 months instead of 1000 days – or something along those lines. Ultimately, I thought I'd listen to the advice, listen to the opinions, but trust that inner voice that spoke to me. So let's see how it goes. The worst thing that can happen is that I don't sell many books. That's not my intention with this book. My intentions are to be able to help those closest to me and provide a tool that will assist my future clients.

By writing down a schedule, you take ownership of your goals; you engrave them into your subconscious. I'm a very big believer that what gets scheduled gets done, so handwriting a schedule is incredibly important to achieving your goals.

I have put together a page of resources you can access yourself so you have systems and templates to get started. I trust you will enjoy this journey. I look forward to hearing about your progress and what you've come away from the book with. I'd love to get your email and hear from those people who achieve their next million dollars in 1000 days. Good luck!

PART 1

Natasa Denman
Up Close and Personal

Chapter 1
Imprint

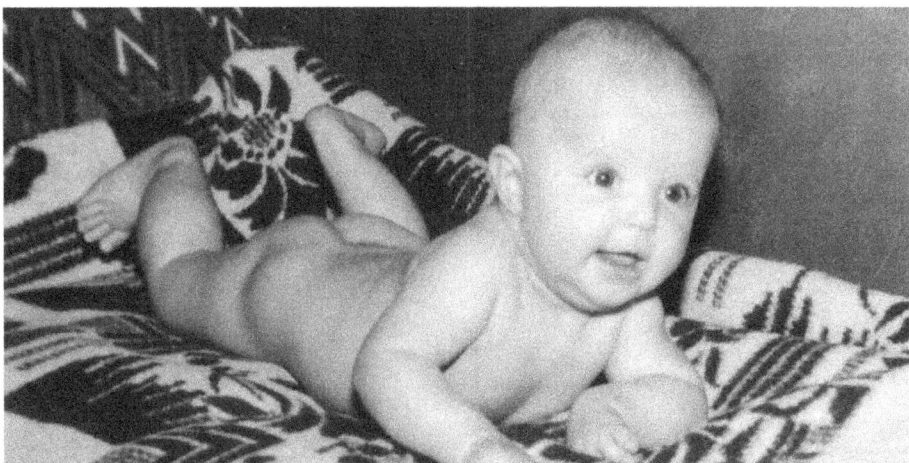

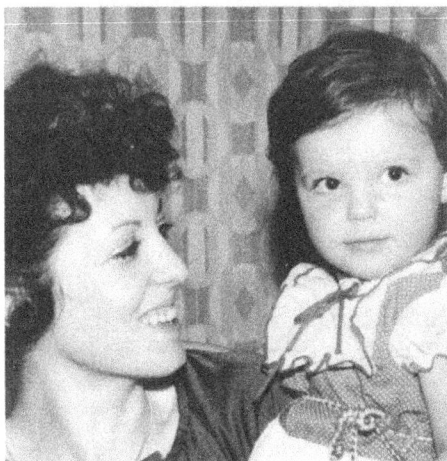

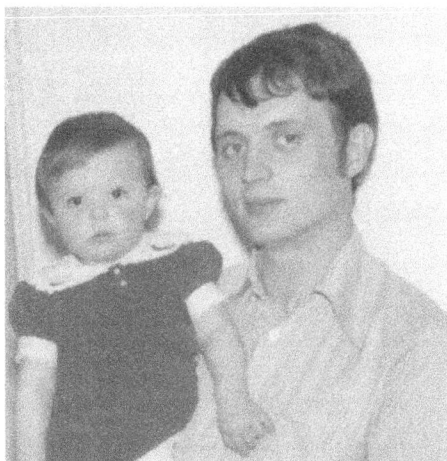

Every beginning is hard. Those were the words from my mum as I was growing up. Those words have made the biggest impact on me on this journey through business, life and learning to be resilient, persistent and independent. For the very first time I have decided to write a little bit about where I grew up and where my beliefs around business, life and personal relationships have come from. I want to share my story thus far, so that when my children grow up they can also learn and read about me and how I used to think and where it all originated.

Un-resourceful strategies, patterns, and strong limiting beliefs had a firm grip on me for many years. In this chapter I want to talk about the part of my life when they were created – my childhood. The age of 0–14 in particular, because those are the years that I spent growing up in Macedonia. I was born in Skopje in 1977, in a completely different culture and way of life to my life now in Melbourne, Australia.

We all can identify with certain moments: things that were said, done and overcome in life. Everyone has a story and this is my story.

My earliest memory goes back to being an 18-month old little girl. People often say you don't remember anything before the age of 3 or 4, but this was a very strong incident that occurred that has been embedded and engraved in my mind with crystal clarity. It was an unfortunate incident that has left a lot of pain. When we experience a lot of pain we tend to remember it a lot more than the moments of love and pleasure early on in our years and for me it was witnessing my father physically abusing and beating my mum.

It happened at my grandmother's house, where my parents lived with the in-laws, as you did in Macedonia then. When you got married the wife moved into the husband's home with his parents. People very rarely were able to afford to move out of home when they got married, so oftentimes three generations were living under the one roof.

My grandma had this couch in the lounge room that had only enough space underneath for a small child to crawl under. It's been very firmly engraved in my mind, watching my dad one day get really angry at my mum. I don't know the real circumstances. He's a very fiery character and one that can snap at the drop of a hat. I can remember him pushing my mum under that particular couch and severely beating her. I was really upset; I kicked and screamed and tried to pull him off her. My grandmother, his mother, came out and picked me up so I wouldn't watch anymore. She did nothing to stop the situation and took me away to another room of the house when all of this was happening. This is the moment I created one of my first beliefs about the kind of relationships I was going to seek out in my life and how I was going to be as a person. At this moment I had decided that women were weak and I would never be with a man like my father. I took on his personality and became him, as he seemed strong, and subsequently married Stuart who has a very similar personality to my mum. He is very nurturing, loving and thoughtful. Yet my mother has continued to attract men in her life similar to her father who was also abusive towards my grandmother. Two very similar fathers with two very different outcomes in what we made it mean for ourselves.

Often what we learn in training and seminars is that we either marry our mums or dads and it's usually the person of the opposite sex that we marry. In this case I moved away from my father and ended up marrying someone similar to my mum and took on some quite strong, stubborn characteristics as well as the business mindset from my dad. My father also has some wonderful qualities, very strong to his word and resourceful in business. He clearly also has the negative traits and weaknesses, which are not to be excused or in any way forgiven. It is what it is and we know that we cannot change people, they can only choose to change themselves and learn from the feedback life gives them.

I have had closure and conversations with him since; I don't agree with what he does, but he's my father at the end of the day and I do love him very much. He lives in Macedonia and we have sporadic contact with him. He married four times and he physically abused all his wives. Oftentimes I would jump in and attempt to rescue them. I have been in that rescuer position in these situations with many of his partners and have worked a lot on myself around clearing those limiting beliefs, which were embedded back then. It wasn't my place to rescue anyone.

My parents ended up divorcing when I was 3 years old and thus began the journey of me being raised by four very strong women. It was my grandma, my mum and her two sisters.

My mum worked three jobs as I was growing up and this is where another limiting belief around building wealth and earning money was created. By watching her work three jobs, I grew up creating the belief that you have to work hard to make lots of money. I watched her go to her day job from 7am–3pm, because in Macedonia they start work at 7am. She'd come home and she'd draw all these crosswords for local media and magazines that used to take photos of them and put them in the magazines. She was a draftsperson and did this really well. At night she'd go and be the bingo call girl till 11pm. She'd sit there and say what numbers were coming up and then she'd come home late. I had to look after myself from a very young age. We lived with my grandma and aunty in the earlier years up until I was 10. After that we bought a 1-bedroom studio apartment where we lived for two years before she migrated to Australia.

In my world my mum has always been a single mum and me an only child. We say we grew up together and oftentimes when we talk about the past we say, 'Remember when we were little…' Because she had me when she was 19, we were both really like children and have grown up together in some respects.

I really needed to break my limiting belief about money: that you've got to work hard to make lots of money. It kept propping it's ugly head up in the first couple of years of my business. I worked my butt off and couldn't break through that $50,000–$70,000 turnover. It kept coming back to the fact that perhaps that was true. Nowadays I don't believe it's true; I work a lot less. I worked a lot less generating the million dollars that we've turned over in the last 12 months than I did in the first couple of years in business. I have busted that limiting belief. I have proven to myself that it was not the truth as I believed it to be.

We lived a middle class life in Macedonia and I was always taught to save money for the big things that I wanted to buy and also to have that built-in buffer. My strong women used to say to me, *save up the money for those black days when unexpected expenses occur*. Nowadays I always have that backup which is great and if something comes up I am not totally lost or hopeless. I still have my independence, which I believe was a great thing to learn from early on. When those unexpected moments in life do occur, I'm ready for them because of this mindset that was instilled in me by my strong women.

Let me introduce you to these four strong women and how I have a little bit of each of them in me.

I'll start with my grandmother. Her name was Kate and she was a very strong woman who raised three daughters and helped her husband run the family business – a lemonade shop. When we were little we used to go to markets and run the lemonade shop as a part of this permanent market. We used to make it from scratch and fill the bottles at home. It was a very popular and profitable business back in those days.

My grandma was the one who upheld the family and kept everyone together even with the abuse and the alcoholism that she had to endure while being with my grandfather. My grandfather and I share the same birthday, so I had picked up a lot of traits from him and my father. They're the people that I subconsciously thought I needed to become in order to thrive and survive in life. Both very social and likeable in their networks and strong providers for their families.

I've always gone around doing things to make my grandma proud. I was her only granddaughter in her life. She lived until the year 2000 and my grandfather passed away when I was only four years old. I can only remember being raised by my grandmother and her three daughters.

My aunty Ema is the eldest of the three sisters and she has got her own successful legal business in Macedonia. She has always been a person who loves to learn, read and is very philosophical about how she views the world. You can have those real deep and meaningful conversations that are very stimulating for the mind with her. She is very wise and from her I believe I always looked up and wanted to have that certain career and to be at a level where I was respected and was also not thinking about money. She has made some very smart investments and knows how to manage herself and has thrived being able to raise two boys as a single mum with a turbulent and successful career and business.

When I look at her, she is always very relaxed about how she spends her money and I notice that she knows what she's got and manages it really well. I wanted to achieve that kind of freedom so I looked up to her a lot and enjoyed the conversations with her very much as they challenge me and get me to see things from a different perspective.

Then comes my auntie Mira. She got polio at the age of 10 months. They were able to save her aside from her right leg. Her right leg below the knee never fully developed, it's always been smaller than the left one. She has walked on a crutch all her life. My auntie Mira is the closest you can get to my personality. She's humorous, social, loves people and nothing stops her. She is a person that has no excuses, even though she's the one that has had the most challenges. She needed to be resilient to overcome bullying because of her disability. All her life she's walked with one crutch, nowadays on two crutches and undergoes operations to make her life easier and reduce pain. Yet she never whinges or whines about herself.

What I've seen in her all my life is that zest for life, that ability to stand up for herself. To say what she wanted and to say whom she wanted to be with. Out of these four women, she has been the one that has always had the most wonderful partners. She never married, however the partners that she's had throughout her life have looked after her and really put her up on a pedestal and she's been treated truly like the queen.

I find that really resembles what I have in my life, because my husband does the same for me and I have also always in the past attracted people who have really looked after me and were just wonderful people to be around. Being with her I learnt how to be around people who are different. In Macedonia, disability was not common, so often you would get looks and stares and uncomfortableness from the public. I see disabled people just slightly differently from everyone else, but they're just as much people and oftentimes they're people who we need to look up to and learn from. They teach us true resilience and persistence, how to get things done in their own unique way, to be very creative and very resourceful.

That's what really impressed me about Mira, so I took on that creativity and outgoingness. She used to work in a bank and taught me about money, savings and how to make sure that I had enough for the future. She's been retired for the last 20 years and she's fully financially independent. Everyone's ultimate goal is to be able to retire without being on a pension, or government support. She still gets some disability support, but most of her income is derived from investment properties, rentals and other things that she's organised herself to make sure that she doesn't have to rely on other people and can get that support for herself.

Just like Robert Kyosaki spoke of in his book *Rich Dad Poor Dad*, I like to say she was like my rich mum, because even though she's not flamboyantly rich she can sustain her life without having to work and have that passive income to support her.

Last of all, my dear mum, who's a very nurturing type of personality and a person that has taught me about sacrifice, resilience, independence and also who has that entrepreneurial spirit herself. I believe her migrating at the age of 31 to a country on the other side of the world where she didn't speak the language was an amazing and courageous move. She came on a tourist visa at the time, to start up a life and to access the education and opportunities that Australia offered.

I see that as her big leap of faith to move across the world and to have sacrificed two and a half years being separated from her child, to set up a life here, so that I could then come over to something permanent. How she ended up staying was that she met my step-dad and they started dating. Nine months later, when she was due to go back to Macedonia, they decided to declare a de facto relationship and that was good enough at the time for the government to grant her that permanent residency.

After that it still took two and a half years to arrive in this country myself. It was the toughest two and a half years because back then we didn't have the ability or couldn't afford those phone calls between Macedonia and Australia. It was something like the equivalent of $50 a minute! So it was letters that we would send back and forth, which took 2–3 weeks to get to each other. As a girl, I missed out on having my mother there as I became a teenager. However the other three strong women in my life looked after me so well and I am so grateful for that. I am grateful for the opportunity that this particular experience gave me.

It wasn't the ideal situation to live for those two and a half years without my mum. What it taught me though was resilience, independence and patience in that time waiting to be reunited with Mum in Australia. It was big learning curve as much as it may not have seemed like anything at the time.

Social life and school in Macedonia was also very different to what it was here in Australia. People over there mainly value fun and being around other people. They work to live, they don't live to work! This is where I've brought that part of me here and this is why the way I have developed the business is very much around the value of fun and people.

Taking people on my Ultimate 48 Hour Author Retreats ties in really nicely with those values I was raised with. An awesome belief I instilled was that the quality of your life is dependent on how many memories and holidays you can take and create with your nearest and dearest. That's the core thing that I have always encouraged to happen in my life. We spend about three months away each year in going to either long weekends away from home, a couple of overseas holidays per year and a big Christmas break. All of those things are super important to me and I value them highly over materialistic things like having a mansion or a Porsche. I prefer to spend my money on memories, trips and experiences over things.

School in Macedonia was hard-core. Over there you tend to do about 15 different subjects in primary school. I finished year 8 before moving here and the quality and the standard of what you learn at that age is 5–6 years ahead of what children learn here in schools. Which meant when I came here I was already ahead in maths, physics, chemistry etc. All of those subjects were so advanced back in Macedonia, that I really did well academically here and persisted and focused mostly on learning to speak English. I achieved a standard of B's in normal English class. I was meant to attend ESL classes (English as a Second Language), but I didn't understand why I was being put into this class so I kept going back to my normal English class and finished off high school in normal English even though I could have gotten better marks doing ESL.

Why did I end up being in business? I believe that history repeats itself, and what I had witnessed growing up in my childhood, was that most of my family were business owners, from the lemonade shop that my grandma and grandfather owned and the businesses that my dad had. My dad had a TV repair business. He was electronically savvy and used to repair people's DVD players, TVs and all sorts of electronic equipment. My grandfather, alongside my dad, had a business within the same shop. He repaired people's shoes for a living. My uncle, dad's brother, also had a business – he was a locksmith. My auntie Ema, had her legal firm. So I was constantly surrounded by my relatives who all had their own businesses. I also got to witness times those businesses were amazing and very abundant, and other times where everyone was sitting quietly, hoping that it will turn around. Similar to nowadays as business is not always going to be on an upward trend. It will go up and down and have those peaks and troughs.

The reason I've ended up doing what I do right now is because that's always the way it's been done and my family has always chosen to live life on their terms and their own time. They have worked very hard and had always been really creative and entrepreneurial. As I mentioned, we were more of a middle class family rather than rich. We had everything we wanted and we went away on all the holidays that we desired to bond and have that quality time together.

Macedonia is a wonderful country. I visit every couple of years on average and I've taken my kids and husband to visit. We have travelled to Greece and we use it as our base and we travel around Europe, which is wonderful as I feel like I am at home when I go back. I can connect and keep in touch with all of my friends, thanks to the power of Facebook and social media. I love having that as my background. I'm proud of it and I like the way it makes me feel when I go back home and get to do things differently than what we do here. It is wonderful, refreshing and it really appeals to my need for variety and adventure.

The last thing I wanted to bring up from my childhood was the words that my dad said about me before I left, which really stuck into my head and something that had made a big difference in how I was going to tackle life moving forward. I was in the spare room at his shop and I could hear him talking to one of his customers. I am guessing he was heartbroken to have me leave the country permanently and not be near him. Nowadays I know that was the real, core issue behind what he said, but at the time I didn't know this.

What he said to his customer that I overheard is this: 'She's going to go over there and she'll become a prostitute.' He had this perception or belief that anyone that goes out to a westernised country turns into a loose girl who ends up being very rebellious and gives up her body to everyone.

Those were the words that really stuck in my mind, but fortunately the person that I am and what I've always continued to do in my life is to prove men wrong about what I was going to turn out to be like. Similar things happened with my stepfather here, where he always thought that once I get out into the real world, things wouldn't be as easy as what I think. Those were not my beliefs – I know that now. I understand those were their beliefs, but it's interesting how it was a protection mechanism of some sort to say that and to be unaware obviously of how things were going to unfold or affect the person you were saying them about.

So those were the words my father left with me before I came here. I have a reasonable relationship with him. We catch up whenever I go there, but not so much while I'm here. There are things that I believe he is very talented at. I've learnt from him, but there are those weak moments where there are irrational actions being taken. I understand that he's doing the best he can with what he's got, and if he knew better he'd do better. So I just choose to respect him as a parent and I know that I also have a lot of his traits within me.

I have to be grateful and there's no love like the love you have for a parent. I believe that I have got traits from both him and my mum. The person that I've become today is partially shaped by what I have observed, heard and experienced in my life. Being encouraged and being told that I am good enough, I can do anything that I set my mind to and that there are people who are proud of me has also shaped me as a person.

Chapter 2
Transition

June 9, 1991, I landed at Tullamarine Airport and arrived via the Yugoslav Airplane Transport in Australia. I was so excited about moving here and being part of this country and culture. Mostly I was very excited to be reunited with my mum, who was at the airport waiting for me, seven months pregnant.

My arrival in Australia was exciting to begin with. After a few weeks I realised how lonely and isolated everyone was from each other. It wasn't that you could go out on the streets and hang out with your friends or go to a coffee shop and have a bit of banter and socialise like I was used to back in Macedonia.

I was surrounded by kids who were still very much school/home, school/home, a little bit of socialising, but nothing like what I had experienced back in Macedonia. Back in Macedonia what we had were nightclubs for under-age kids and it was not a written rule, but people under-age used to go out in the earlier hours, say from 7–11pm and then people over 18 would come out quite late. Over there anyone over 18 doesn't start to get ready until till 10pm at night, which is just the way the culture is.

My arrival in Australia was an exciting yet huge change and even though my mum always taught me that every beginning is hard, I felt very alone. The TV was my best friend; shows like *Neighbours* and *Home & Away* were my friends. I experienced a few ups and downs in my early friendships with people here. I felt betrayed and lied to by a couple of people who thought they could take advantage of the fact that I didn't know too much about how to be in this country.

I was strong though and persisted. I focused on my studies, did really well academically, because the way we got taught back in Macedonia was much more advanced in the early stages of primary and high school than it was here. I got involved in a lot of academic activities. Debating was one of the things that I was part of. I went to public school, (Kew High School) and was one of five members in our debating team. I hardly spoke English, however

I used to be always the first speaker to set up the argument for the team so what I used to do is memorise my whole speech for delivery as I didn't have the ability to rebut on the spot.

That's where my training in public speaking started. I learned to manage my nerves and practice being in front of people. I believe that was a foundation that I created back then for my future in speaking. It was the very first time a public school entered a debating team to compete against all private schools. We were the true underdogs. We ended up blowing everyone away and ended up getting to the round of 16 in the state finals, amongst other very competitive and high-quality teams.

That was a proud moment for our school especially and we were celebrities at our school for many years to come. The school subsequently entered other teams who had very little or no success in reaching the finals.

Another important event of my adolescent years was that I got to run a mock-up business/company that was being mentored by employees of Vic Roads. The program was called Young Achievers Australia and 5 different schools put 3–4 students into this particular group. Our mentors taught us how to start a company from scratch, how to build it, sell some shares and ultimately create a product to sell. If the product was successful and we were in profit then we would return to shareholders a profitable outcome on their original purchase of shares or no outcome at all.

I stepped into this particular program with 25 other students from 5 different schools in our area. It was Year 11 and we were all around 16–17 years old. At the beginning of the program people were asked to select what positions they would like to take. The company we were creating was a proper company – it had the administrative, manufacturing, marketing, human resources, and general management functions.

I – being a high achiever who likes the spotlight – decided to back myself and put my hand up for the general manager role. I thought if I don't put my hand up to do the role that I really want to do, the answer will always be 'no'. Many of the other students were scared and had that feeling of not being good enough. I thought, there's nothing to lose here, so I did put my hand up to become the general manager and take on that leadership and responsibility role for our company.

There were three people in total who put their hand up and then we got voted in. We presented ourselves and our arguments. I got the role and over the next six months I was coordinating the whole company with the mentoring by the employees from Vic Roads.

This particular role was an integral part about me taking responsibility and putting myself in a leadership position. And let me tell you, did I have a lot of responsibility and did I do a lot of work! Not only did I do the general manager's work, but I believe I put in so much work in the other areas so that we would succeed. We called the company Hypa, which was an interesting choice for a business name and very reflective of my personality and amount of energy I put into things.

Our product was the creation of four different colours of boxer shorts. If you remember back in the 90s, boxer shorts were huge for sleeping in at night especially the satin ones. As I was so determined to make this company successful, I wanted to make sure that everything was handled and coordinated correctly, to the point where my mum was helping me cut out these boxer shorts before they were sent off for sewing and manufacturing. We did quite a lot of things ourselves to make sure it was a success. We sold $2 shares to our family and friends from the 25 students and in the end the outcome was that we had 200% profit, which meant every shareholder got double their money back. Funnily enough, a lot of our shareholders said they wished they'd bought more shares at the beginning.

It was a really wonderful learning experience and journey and something that I look back on. We even went to the point of producing an annual report, with all the pictures. We used to run meetings and call our shareholders in and tell them where we were over that 6-month period. I ran all of these events and we even got some publicity. The pictures at the start of this chapter illustrate some of the times with Hypa.

This is where a positive resourceful belief was created around me being able to step up, take responsibility and become a leader. This is what I always say to people, as people often shy away from that leadership position, because it requires responsibility. It can be a lonely place to be, where you can find other people don't like what you're doing or they don't agree and resonate with what you're saying. Your responsibility though lies in backing yourself because the rewards at the end are so much greater than in any other position.

Over my adolescent years I did go back to Macedonia regularly. I really did miss my friends and people I had gone to school with and grown very close to. I went back on average every 2–3 years for a few months over the summer holidays and it was really great to continue nurturing those relationships with people. I think I'm the only person that I know who goes often just to nurture those relationships. I believe it's core to my personality that I want to keep in touch. I have a desire to know what's going on in other people's lives and vice versa and have a great time.

When I finished high school successfully, I decided to enrol into a Bachelor of Applied Science – Psychology and Psychophysiology. This was a double major at Swinburne University in Melbourne. It was a three-year degree, which I chose because I simply loved to learn more about human behaviour. I loved uncovering why we do certain things and what keeps us going and what puts blocks in front of us. Nowadays, knowing what I know, being a coach and a mentor was always a much better fit for me than say going into the more clinical side of things such as counselling.

Nevertheless it still played a big role in my evolution. Everything has played a part and culminated in the results and strengths I have today.

Overall my adolescence was up and down, more down in the early days, especially between age 14 and 16 during the transition and the adjustment period to becoming an Australian citizen. Australia is one of the most wonderful places and I'm so grateful that my mum brought me here where I have so many opportunities my peers in Macedonia do not. It's very disheartening to see people that I studied with living very tough lives over there – being and feeling stuck.

I'm a big believer that you are in charge of your destiny and unfortunately the mindset over there is geared towards scarcity and that in order for someone to win, someone else has to lose and vice versa. This is sad to see and it tends to feed through a lot of the culture. Every time I go back, people are saying things are worse and worse. When they talk about their careers and complain about the political situation of the country the answer is that everything is getting worse and worse and it is someone else's fault that they are struggling. Yet when I actually look at how they interact, how everyone has an annual holiday and everyone is able to come up with resources to have a good time and socialise, I can see it's untrue.

The language they choose to use is not the best and it's no wonder they are not thriving but just surviving. When I visit, all I can do is be there and listen, but I cannot change anyone's life unless they're willing to step up themselves.

I look forward to now sharing with you the adult side of Natasa Denman and what evolved over the decade before I started my business and the defining moments that have occurred that contributed to building and creating what it is today. Every part of the journey has its own purpose and its own reason why it's occurred, and absolutely nothing actually happens by mistake as it is preordained and set up so that the future outcome is what it was destined to be. Life is perfect!

Chapter 3
Growth

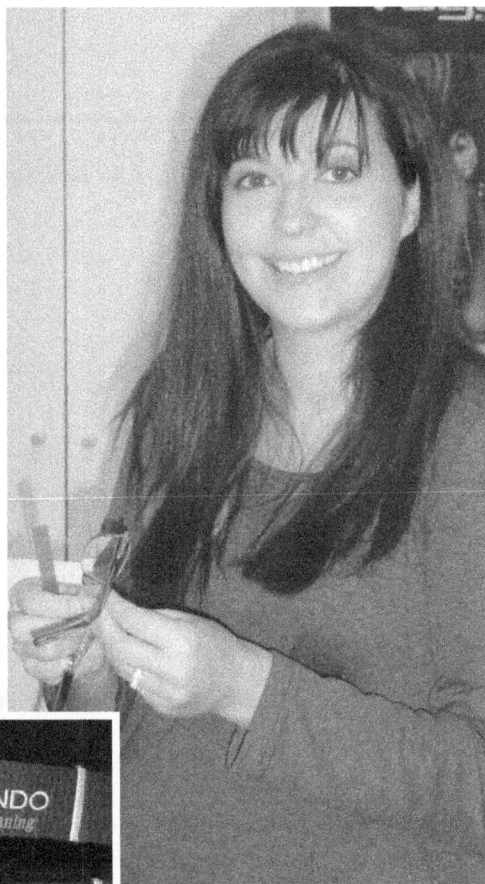

In my life thus far, I have only ever had three jobs. My very first job was working in a comic book store. I spent five years there. My second job was with a big retailer in the optical industry.

In the comic book store I took real pride in my environment, how I organised myself in what I was doing and the systems that I put in place. If you can imagine tens of thousands of different comics, magazines, action figures and things like that needed to be visually merchandised. Luckily I did not have any interest in those products that we were selling, so I focused on getting the job done and making the store look as presentable as possible while the other staff were consumed by playing with the merchandise. This is where I noticed that I was very systematic in the way I got things done. I got that feedback from my employer and my manager always said he loved when I worked, because I would leave the place in very good order and well-organised for the next person who was coming in.

While I was working in the comic book store, I also studied a diploma at the Northern Metropolitan Institute of Technology. I completed a diploma in Information Technology because I thought computers were the way of the future, and this could only be of benefit in time. I also wasn't ready to take on a full time job, so I got a second job in the optical industry in a very large company and ended up spending a decade there. I worked a long time in Melbourne and then moved to New Zealand for a year and very quickly was able to reach a managerial position in New Zealand.

I was one of the youngest managers to take on a store that was generating $2 million turnover per year. This was a huge learning curve as I was young and inexperienced in managing people, especially the challenging personalities that were working with me at the time. Nevertheless, it was a wonderful opportunity so that when I returned to Melbourne I was put into a managerial position straight away. It was a lot more competitive back in Melbourne and those positions were held and only offered to people twice my age as they had been with the company for 20–30 years.

It was a back door entry and a great way to progress in my career in optics. I was always looking for new challenges and to grow in the stores I managed. I always say that I treated those stores as if they were my own businesses. I remember spending five years in one particular store where the turnover was only $250,000 and it was a one-man show with an optometrist. I managed to increase that store's turnover to $1 million within three years with only a little bit of help from a part-time staff member.

When I finished up there, I was promoted to a large store in a very affluent suburb and I was managing 15 staff with a turnover of $5 million dollars. Working in the optical industry, learning and understanding how to manage people, giving customer service at a world-class level for maximum client retention and return was very important to me. I learned to understand the numbers, the reports, wages to sales, cost of goods and the bottom line in terms of what profit we were running at. Those profit and loss reports were something that I used to digest regularly to make sure that we were achieving our key performance indicators. I ended up winning 'store of the year' one of the years, which was a big highlight from the time I was with this company.

That's also how I met my husband Stuart. We met at a conference as he was also a fellow manager of a different store and we began going out from 2004. We have been together just over a decade now and have three beautiful children. As time went on, we ended up deciding to purchase a third-owned franchise into a different, big, optical retailer that moved into Australia in the year that I was about to have my first baby. Stuart bought that franchise and it became his business as I was going on maternity leave for the following 12 months.

It was an exciting time in our lives, as we wanted to produce extra income through generating profit from our own business as well as our salaries. I always looked at how I could challenge myself, grow more, push myself to the next level rather than just settling for an 'X' amount of salary per year and just being happy with that.

During the time that I went out with Stuart I also got my black belt in Taekwondo. This was a great achievement after finishing the diploma in IT. The love for learning and being involved in different courses, growing my intellectual property and skill set has always been with me. I have never spent too much time without being part of some course or an educational institution where I was completing a certain degree, or improving my skills.

Throughout my twenties and my adult years I always attracted nice men as partners and I have never had any bad break-ups. I think that was because of that belief that I was always looking out for that person that resembled more my mother than my father. I've been blessed in that way, unlike some of my friends who always tended to attract people who were disrespectful and hurtful towards them.

The time came and Stuart and I chose to invest in our first property. Soon after, we got pregnant with our first child and decided to get married. We did everything in reverse order. Becoming a parent was a real life-changing moment, as those of you who are parents would know. Everything seemed totally different and I started to view the world through a different set of eyes.

It was really tough to begin with. It didn't quite take me the two years I normally say it takes me to get used to something brand new, however it did take me a good 6–7 intense months to get used to being a mum. Oftentimes I would sit there and ask myself, why did I decide to do this? In hindsight, it's the best thing I've ever done. I am also about to have my third baby (tomorrow!) as I'm finishing up this book. This is the last chapter I chose to write while awaiting the arrival of our third child.

Our children have brought so much joy and happiness in our lives and have taught us further responsibility and unconditional love. They are so beautiful. Each and every one of them is unique and I'm sure this third one is going to be just as amazing and unique. We love them the most in the world, it binds our family and its so much fun and an adventure as we all grow and change throughout our lives. I'm so blessed and happy to have had my healthy and thriving children. My husband's the most wonderful father out there, who looks after them and me, because I'm not much of a cook. He truly has taken on that support role so that I can work to keep our lifestyle at the level that it is and to satisfy my own core needs of growth, significance and variety, which I crave.

Our biggest change and challenge occurred in March 2010 when something really big happened that I was not aware of. As I was working part-time in a different franchise from the one we owned, I got a phone call from my husband who said: "Please leave everything that you're doing and come home. Juddy is okay, just come home, I need to tell you something."

That really stressed me out because I had no idea what was happening. I picked up my stuff and went into my car. The drive from the store to home was just five minutes, part of the reason I chose to work there part-time. I thought, *oh my god, something's happening, my mum or Stuart's dad is probably sick or dead*. As I was driving home it felt like the longest five minutes. I picked up my phone and rang my mum. She picked up, which was a relief and was not sure what was going on either. I arrived home to see my husband as I walked through the front door with his face in his hands on the floor in the lounge room. I still had no idea, maybe he was sick or not well. He just said, "I lost the business."

Initially I felt a great sense of relief, because it was nothing to do with being unwell. The enormity of the situation didn't come to me until a few hours later. He said he had made a very poor decision and we had lost the business instantly. There was nothing that could be done. He just said, "I have nowhere to go tomorrow."

Thus the process of having the worst moment in my life began. Shit hit the fan and I went through the usual stages of denial, anger, blame, depression and ultimately acceptance and resurgence. Exactly how I had studied it in my psychology days. Luckily, I'm the type of person who does things very quickly and I went through the whole array of emotions in 3–6 weeks. I sought out some counselling. I went and chatted to someone for a few sessions, and in the third session I walked in and declared that I was going to be a life coach. So my journey into this new world was decided and declared back then.

Little did I know that this journey was going to be about further helping and healing me. I had to get through what had happened so I could then start helping other people overcome their own challenges. I decided to take responsibility for my future, financial independence and safety. I have always been a bit of a control freak and what I've discovered is that the core reason around that has been because I haven't felt safe. Most of my life and I have watched those four strong women of mine whom I grew up with also fight for themselves and their financial security and independence in life. With my husband losing the business and making that poor decision, I felt unsafe especially having a child to look after and a second one on the way at the time.

I became a coach and very quickly realised that coaching is very much a tool and not the whole business itself. We actually need to solve a common problem that people have and are willing to spend money to have solved. We use our coaching skills as part of our life toolbox, which we have alongside strategies and ideas we can share.

During the past 1000 days, I have learnt a lot about myself. I have become calmer and relaxed and less emotional. All of this because I have learnt to understand how people work and that not everyone's going to be the way that I am. I believe there are not many people out there like me and have realised that one of my biggest drivers is doing things fast and at the same time having a lot of fun. My most important values are business and money as they take care of my values of family and home. That is why I made certain sacrifices especially in the first two years, so that I would be able to provide the lifestyle that I envision for myself and my family.

I outgrew a lot of people that I hung out with in life in those first couple of years. I was totally okay with that, because my direction, focus and values changed. They shifted dramatically and I created new relationships through the networks that I started joining and the people I started talking to more and more often. When you have things in common with people you tend to develop the relationship and that closer bond a lot quicker. I regularly reflect on my decisions and emotions. If something really annoys me, frustrates me or I enjoy it, I reflect upon it to understand myself better. My husband and I do this together. I am able to self-coach myself out of some frustrating situations because I have a deeper understanding of myself.

I have realised that as a business owner and entrepreneur your life will never be in balance. I don't believe there's such a thing as balance, where you're spending eight hours sleeping, eight hours on your business and eight hours on your life to make up those 24 hours. I believe there is a flow that can be achieved amongst everything that we're doing so that our life gets lived through the business and the business supports our life in wonderful ways. I'm all about achieving that flow and having fun with it and not working traditional hours.

I don't have to work specific hours. I love sleeping in and staying up late to be creative. I have a lot of flexibility. When I focus and work, sometimes I can have long days and long nights and many days in a row and other times there's complete freedom. We travel, we're not home on average 3 months out of the year and travel to wonderful destinations and have weekends away, so that we can reconnect and have that quality time, rather than quantity time.

People often ask me – do you ever stop? I say, not really, my vocation is my vacation, so when I am working in my business, on my business, with my clients, I feel like I'm on vacation. Often, I pinch myself because I actually get paid to do this. It's so much fun. I'm enjoying helping people and at the same time it is my career, my vocation and how I get the cash flow to help my family and others. When I pick up that laptop or iPad, answer an e-mail and go on Facebook or other social media platforms to connect with my people and nurture those relationships, it's not hard.

I do it because I want to not because I need to. I have choice. When you get your business to that level where you are completely in that 'want to do this' space because you are enjoying what you're doing so much, then you don't have to work another day in your life. There are days when I feel like I'm working, I have to agree with that. Eighty per cent of the time I don't feel like I'm working. I feel like I'm just hanging out, enjoying the company of people, talking to them and helping them solve their problems.

That has been my adulthood thus far, how I've progressed through the years beyond my twenties since I moved out of home. Everything I've done so far has been the foundation on which I built a million-dollar coaching business from home in 1000 days. I believe every single job/role that I was part of taught me something about myself, how to run a business effectively, successfully, how to look after customers and clients and be organised so when those busy times hit, I can handle it and continue to provide the same service without compromise.

I trust that this has been insightful for you. This journey is about to get even more exciting and fun especially with our new member of our family joining us soon. Most likely in the next 24 hours! At the end of my life, I know I will look back and be content and happy with how it's all unfolded and the legacy I have left, not just for others I have helped, but for my family and for people who are looking to recreate this journey for themselves.

PART 2

Journey to a
Million Dollars

Chapter 1
Shortcut

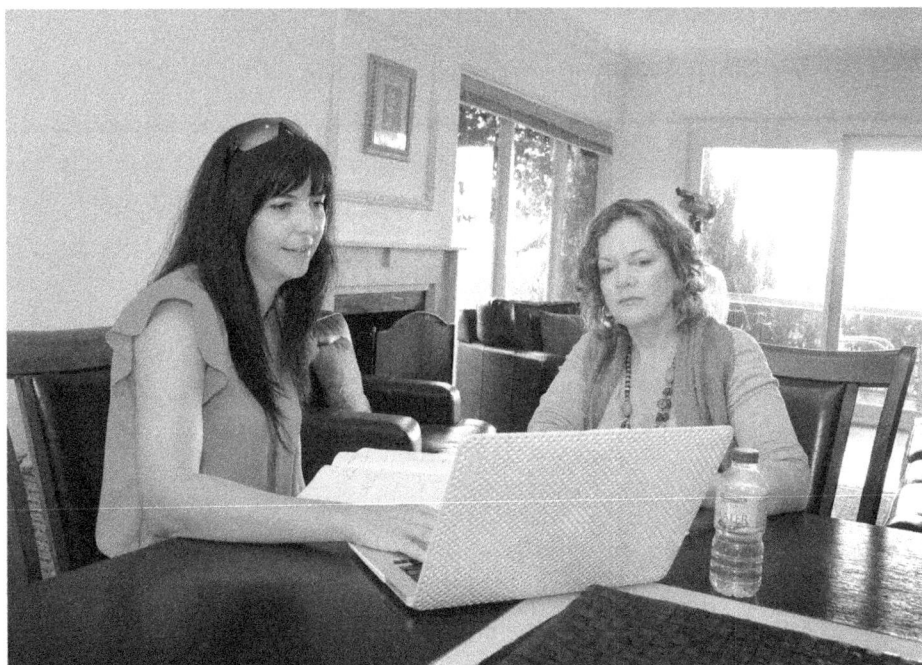

*"Mentoring is a brain to pick, an ear to listen, and a push
in the right direction."*
– John C. Crosby

So you want a shortcut? You're looking for that recipe for success, and you want to get there as quickly as possible. There certainly are shortcuts as much as it may not seem like it at the time. What I'm talking about here is mentoring, gaining education from experts, and investing in systems that will get you there the fastest way possible.

I'm a very big fan of having a coach and a mentor on your journey to success especially in business, because success in business is just like a university degree. You need to learn the different steps that you need to take, you must achieve a certain mindset when you're learning how to do it and overcome those challenges and setbacks that come along the way.

Three months into officially starting up my business, I had hired my very first mentor, and it was the very best decision that I made. I had heard people say that having a coach or a mentor on your journey gets you from A to B the fastest way possible.

I relayed that to my husband and said to him, I don't know how we're going to find the money. I was already investing in a couple of other programs from which I was gaining education on how to build my business and also fine-tune my own coaching skills. But we did, we made some sacrifices and I was able to hire my first mentor.

Without any doubt I can now say with confidence that it's definitely the quicker road to success. As much as it seemed futile in the first year. Mentors have already done what you want to do. They can provide the steps and the answers, which can assist you to get to the next point. Having a mentor on your journey does not guarantee you won't make mistakes, but you will avoid many that you might otherwise make if you try to do it on your own.

The support, encouragement and wisdom that you get from them will lead you to success. The trick with mentors and having people assisting you on the journey is to be able to trust and follow through on their advice. Did you know that 95% of new business owners see mentoring as a cost and not an investment? Therefore they fail to make the decision to get one on their journey and alongside that decision their businesses fail within 1–2 years.

Or some of them try someone out for two to three months and say it doesn't work because they haven't seen any cash flow come through. So there you go, it's no wonder that 9 out of 10 businesses will fail in the first 12 months. When you start out in business, it's really too hard to see the fruits of your labour, even though you may be working 60, 70 or 80 hours per week.

There is a certain amount of infrastructure that you need to set up and a lot of mindset funk that you need to get over to get to those cash flow rewards. I worked with my first mentor for five months before I got my first paying client. That's 150 days! I worked with him on a weekly basis. So I had him for about 20 sessions before I got my first paying client.

In the subsequent 300 days, I only had 3 clients in total. I barely scraped through $7,000 dollars in my first 365 days in business. Business is a marathon, not a sprint and setting the foundations and building the infrastructure are essential steps even though the time you invest doesn't seem to make money.

If you don't get a mentor, you will stagnate in growth, I can guarantee you that. You will waste tons of money and time, along the way. You will take a lot of guesses, you will make a lot more mistakes and worst of all is that you will be driven to quit due to a poor mindset and because there's no one there on the side to pep talk you through the tough times, the stress, the anxiety, and the money and family disturbances that you may experience due to lack of results.

There are a few different things I want you to consider within this chapter: whether you should hire a mentor, coach or a consultant. These are 3 different types of professionals that can help you along your journey. My very first mentor was more of a coach. I believe businesses under a hundred thousand dollars need more coaching, because it is working on those underlying limiting beliefs and overcoming a lot of mental stuff that comes up on the journey.

It is very useful that the coach also has some mentoring experience, whereby they have the results that you want to achieve and they can give you the best of both worlds. That is why when I work with people, I like to say that I am of both of those. I certainly do not implement strategies for my clients, like a consultant would.

If you hire a coach who does not have the business experience on how to build your specific business because they haven't done it before it might end up being a slower journey. That is why I love when coaching is used as a tool within mentoring.

Within this chapter I will talk about mentoring a lot more than coaching, because that is more my style. I love working with clients who I can show the steps to so they go out and execute them, and we can also talk about mindset as it comes up. So, how do you hire and who do you hire as a mentor? Hire those who have the results you want to achieve.

When I was working with my very first mentor, I very much looked for someone who had built a 6-figure business as a coach. Those were the results I was looking to achieve. With him, I not only worked on the start-up foundation strategy of building infrastructure and niching myself, but we also dealt with a lot of the mindset matter that used to come up for me.

With my second mentor, we took it up another notch. I had then gotten to that 6-figure level but I needed to automate a lot of my systems to be able to grow further and generate multiple six figures within the business. With this particular mentor we worked a lot more on sequencing, setting up campaigns and building a community and tribe around what we were doing. This got us to a never-ending list of referrals and people coming to us because they were getting a lot of value from us.

Finally, with our third mentor, it almost went a little bit in the reverse and that was in order to get the business to the 7 figures we needed to be able to create a lot of value, high-value offerings as well as learn some new sales strategies, tips and tricks. We did a lot of change work within ourselves to allow us to grow to that very next level and be able to have a team of people that were able to help us leverage to that point.

To be working and turning a million dollars within your business from home, you need a lot more than just a couple of people on your team. Some of those people will not necessarily be people who are fully employed by you, but could be a virtual assistant who is helping you remotely.

We have a publicity person who helps us with our press releases, a website person who helps us with landing pages and our ad campaigns on social media, and a copywriter. When you are able to have a team of people that you can access in their area of expertise really makes a difference to your bottom line and how you come across as a professional business in the public eye.

When you have a mentor, the number one thing is to follow the recipe. Follow the recipe of what they encourage you to do and what they tell you the next steps for you are. Do not try to re-invent the wheel because these are people who have already achieved what you want to achieve, and by following the recipe and taking action, you are 95% of the way there.

Finally, just stick it out. As I said before, business success is a marathon, not a sprint. Mentors are not miracle workers and you are 100% responsible for your actions and the follow through when it comes to your business success. Think about it this way, you get out what you put in to that journey.

I want to give you 8 essential tips on how to use your mentor to his or her full capacity. So many clients that I have met and even mentored myself do not use their investment in their mentor to its full potential.

I have always told each and every one of my three mentors on my journey that if I hire them, I have made the commitment to myself to take the actions of that they suggest I do. If you have a block around deciding whether to hire a mentor or not, it is never a matter of whether you have the time or money. It is a matter of whether you are committed to following the directions the mentor gives you. Am I backing myself to be stretched and uncomfortable?

Here are my tips on using your mentor:

1. Don't wait for them to chase or call you. If you need help, you contact them. I am sure that your mentor will have other clients that they are looking after and they are responding to. This is why, if I need help, I always ask for it. When I don't, I don't ask for it. Earlier in your journey you may require a mentor a lot more, and later on you will become more independent.

2. Don't waste your money if you're not going to follow their instructions and advice. This goes back to what I said before. Mentoring is an investment. Back yourself, commit on the journey, because you will do the work. Otherwise, don't bother wasting your money.

3. Come prepared to your sessions with questions to get the most value. Don't expect to just be spoon-fed. I have to say, on my journey, I've had a handful of clients who would come in to the sessions and it would be like pulling teeth to work out what they wanted.

    I have been a very big initiator in terms of asking for advice. *Should I be doing this or that? What do you think about this?* I get very creative with the whole process.

4. Discuss ideas with your mentor before following through with them. Your mentor will work out whether your idea is worth pursuing or perhaps putting on the bench for a little while and pursuing later. It might simply be a bad idea. They might tell you not to do it at all. Don't waste your time and money by executing ideas, especially if you have your mentor there to instruct you.

5. Share your successes and your challenges with your mentor. They are not just there for you to whine to. They love to hear when you have those wins and successes along the way because it makes their job a lot more rewarding. They can share in that with you and encourage you more, which fuels you even more towards achieving more successes and wins on your journey.

6. Trust them 100%! If you don't, you're not likely to have the shift and changes you are after. When you trust them 100% your results will show how you have changed.

    I always said, especially to my very last mentor, who was doing some very funky change work with myself and my husband, 'I'm not sure what you're doing here and I don't know how it's working, but I decided when I invested in you that I was going to trust you 100%.I believe that whatever you have been doing has been working on a cellular level.' The results with this particular mentor were that we generated over $300,000 dollars in sales in just 6 weeks. Something was working …

7. Understand it takes time to build your business, and there are 4 stages of business growth. There is infrastructure that takes time to be built. Results follow when this infrastructure is there and when your mindset has shifted from one level to another.

    The mindset required to build a 0 to $50,000 dollar business is different from $50,000 to a $100,000. Then it's different from a

$100,000 to multiple hundreds of thousands, and then again to get to that 7-figure turnover.

8. Don't get advice from other mentors while working with the one that you have hired. One of my favorite sayings is, 'A confused mind will always say no'. There are many different ways to skin a cat. Everyone will always have an opinion and it's not going to be right or wrong, it's just going to be a different opinion.

If you have chosen to work with someone, follow their opinion and what they're advising. I put the blinkers on and just go on and do what my mentor has advised.

There may have been a few things that have arisen for you by reading this chapter. One of the most common things that I hear people come up with is that they can't afford a mentor. Can you afford to spend 10 times the amount of time to get to the success that you want? I'm sure with persistence you will get to the success you want. Time is limited and money is unlimited. Not the other way around. Take that on as your belief.

People think that time is unlimited and money is limited, but it truly is the other way around. If you want something bad enough, you will always find a way. There is always a way, just make sure you understand where your business actually sits on your values list because whatever is higher on your list of values is where you will invest your time and money.

Then there are those who are wary of what their mentor might say. You don't have to always agree with what they say, but if you do go and do what you want and it doesn't work, go back and do what your mentor told you the first time.

There is an interesting quote that often appears on social media, 'If you go and do what you've decided to do and it doesn't work, go back and do what your coach told you to do the first time.' I have been in this situation. I have avoided the advice of my coach/mentor because I haven't wanted to stretch or challenge myself and then realised in time that I should have followed his advice. They can see what you can't, so trust them 100%.

I never actively seek out a mentor. I never interview mentors. They turn up when I'm ready. As long as you're open to the idea and you want the support, the right mentor for you will turn up. They will also turn up when you need to take the next step and grow again.

The day you meet them, you will know that they would be suitable mentors. It has happened to me three times – finding a mentor without intentionally pursuing one. It's not about asking, 'Who is better for me?' or choosing from this person to that. It's about allowing that person to come into my life and telling myself I need someone to get me to the next level in my business, and soon after I am connected to them.

As a result of reading this chapter and the subsequent chapters that are ahead of you, I would love you to give yourself the 3 actions you need to take as a result of what you have read.

I trust that I have shared many insights into mentoring about why it is so important to have mentors on your journey, especially if you want to get a 7-figure business in 1000 days. Here's your chance. Write down the 3 things you will take into action as a result of reading of this chapter.

3 Actions I Commit to Taking to Create my Million Dollar Business		
		Done ✔
1		
2		
3		

Chapter 2
Community

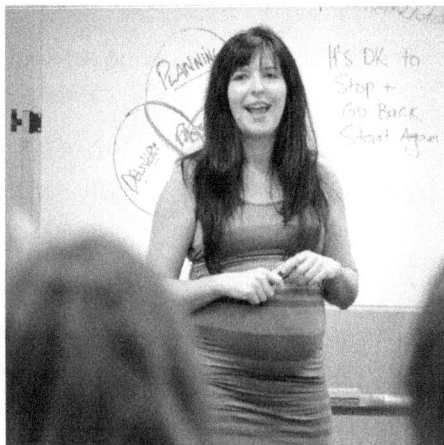

"The richest people in the world look for and build networks, everyone else looks for work."
– Robert Kiyosaki

One of my favourite sayings is, 'Your network equals your net worth.' If you want to get to a 7-figure business, the absolute key will be the relationships you build and nurture over a period of time. It is relationships that build businesses. This is where trust, intimacy and awareness are created around what you do. As more and more people find out who you are and know you on a personal level you will see those relationships transform into business success and increased cash-flow.

People want to know how much you care before they want to know how much you know. When you go out networking, your credibility and positioning increases, especially if you are being consistent in being out there. This was my very next step in line with hiring my mentor that I implemented as one of my key business building activities. To this day it also proves to be the best return on investment of my time and money.

It wasn't something that worked for me initially, however, it built my confidence and clarity around the niche for my very first brand. It helped me to be seen, heard and then liked.

The benefits of networking are that you get to surround yourself by people who are looking to achieve similar results to you, even if they're in different industries. At the same time, you get access to professionals that you need assistance and advice from like bookkeepers, accountants or lawyers. Oftentimes they share advice and some insights for free.

In your early days, when you are low on cash and rich in time you should be filling up your diary as if you had a full book of clients as a coach. If you don't focus on making networking part of your activities in your business then you will end up being very haphazard in the way of becoming known in your community. Not many people will remember you, there will be a lot less word of mouth and lack of referrals coming your way. It will definitely take longer for your business to take off. In line with that, being a coach, a consultant or a mentor, your communication skills around what you do will stagnate. From networking, amazing opportunities arise. Don't miss out on these and the complementary advice that just comes with the territory.

There are two different ways to network and build a community around you. One is online and the other offline. In this chapter, we are going to talk about offline networking. Online networking and building your list will be covered later.

In reality, offline networking will work for you first. I always tell people to become well-known offline before you focus on their online strategy. I see time and time again, coaches and practitioners who want to develop e-courses and online resources and try to sell them with no success because no one knows them from a bar of soap. When you get known offline first, people will look you up online and get interested in the other things that you offer.

That's been my journey and experience. I have seen many struggle for 12 to 18 months and then come to the realisation that they need to get out and hit the pavement. I've got three essential tips I want to share with you to give you the necessary skills on how to become an effective and profitable networker.

Number one is turn up consistently. I'm a big believer that you should pick and trial a few different networking groups and then choose the two that you want to join. When you become a member of a group, it allows you to catch up with the same people regularly, which means it builds that relationship and trust, and allows you to know each other over a longer period of time.

Another essential ingredient required beyond being in a room at an event with many people are those one-on-one coffee chats. They can occur online, after you've met someone offline or they happen in a real coffee shop where you sit down and have a chat to each other face to face. My rule of thumb is always to be attending two networking events every week and catching up with at least a couple of people week in and week out.

Your business growth will be dependent on how many conversations you can generate each and every week. Not everyone that you speak to will be a potential client, but you never know where you might discover some strategic alliances, joint venture partners and people who know people that are your ideal clients.

Consistency is key. You need to learn to love it. You may feel awkward to begin with, walking into a room of strangers who seem to know what they are doing, but there will be new people there that most likely will be in the same boat as you.

Number two is connect online after your offline meetings and ask people for permission to stay in touch via your database or newsletter. A good tip from Donna Brown is to say, 'I really want to stay in touch. Feel free to add me to your database. In turn, would you like me to add you to mine?' When you tell someone that you want them to add you to their database, the law of reciprocity says that off course they'll say yes and ask you to add them to yours as well. After all, if the information is not relevant, after a period of time, any one of you can unsubscribe from each other's lists.

I always look people up on Facebook and LinkedIn when I have met them offline at a networking event. I may go into a room and meet 20 or 30 different people, but I will only connect with the ones that I have had a brief one-on-one conversation with during that event. Sometimes you get access to everyone's business cards, but you won't necessarily have that connection with them enough to then connect online.

Only connect with those people who you know will remember you and will say yes to being a connection on LinkedIn or Facebook. Send them a little message to say it was lovely to meet them or a follow-up email within 48 hours of the event. If you leave it much longer than 48 hours don't even bother.

The most powerful way to connect and follow up is through a real phone call. You pick up the phone and say, 'Hey, I'm just calling to connect with you after our meeting last night – everyone seems to be doing the online thing! I wanted to make a proper connection to say it was lovely to meet you. I trust that we can collaborate in the future and get to know each other better.' You just never know what that may result in – the next conversation or coffee chat, or it might just be 'Lovely to meet you and see you later.'

Number three. When it comes to building a community and networks, there is the need for real focus on helping and educating, rather than pitching and pushing. It has been said many times before that networking is like farming, not hunting. When you're farming, you are planting seeds, look after them, water them and nurture over a period of time. Hunting assumes you're going for the kill straightaway.

Focus on helping and making new friends because friends like each other, help one another and want to do business with each other. My intention at each and every event is to make 2 or 3 close connections with people that I have had some time to speak to and follow up and connect consistently to nurture those connections.

Be a business card collector rather than a business card giver. That way, the ball is in your court. You can follow up and have a strategy to actually build that relationship with people you meet.

I know some of you may not be a people person. I know a part of my personality is that I'm very social and I love being around people as they give me lots of energy.

If you're a coach, consultant or a mentor, I want you to remember this: people buy people. They see an aspect within you that they want for themselves when they are hiring you as a mentor, coach or a consultant. You can become a people person if you really give it a go. Visiting the same groups and focusing on fewer but stronger bonds will ultimately help you to expand that network through the networks they have.

You don't necessarily need to know hundreds of thousands of people. Focusing on a few strong bonds that you can leverage with time is another way of reaching out to more people. You may be terrified to walk into a room full of strangers. So was I. Even being a people person and a social butterfly, I was also terrified because of my deep need to be liked.

You may be fresh in business and believe people won't take you seriously. Everything is awkward before it becomes easy. As Susan Jeffers says in her book, 'Feel the fear and do it anyway.' You will find yourself to be surrounded by people who have been in business for a while, but I can guarantee you that there will also be lots of newbies. Learn from the experienced networkers and grow with those at the same stage as you, supporting each other along the way.

You will never attract people that you are not ready to speak to. I am a big believer in that because I have witnessed it time and time again. The more I grow, the more confidence I build around what I stand for. The more I have worked on building my profile, the higher quality people I attract and the higher quality conversations I end up having. The ones that I attracted earlier on were the right ones for me at the time.

Networking does consume a lot of time. Don't look at it as a cost, but an investment. When you go out networking in the real world, you are building that closer bond a lot quicker with people. What will take you 10 to 12 touch points online will take perhaps 2 to 3 or even shorter in real life, the more confident you become in building rapport and yourself.

When I started out, I would need to see people 5 to 7 times before I felt really comfortable chatting to them and being really friendly. Nowadays, I walk in and the second time I see someone it feels like we have really gotten to know each other. It is about becoming a faster rapport builder. Assuming rapport is assuming that everyone you meet is going to like you, which is a much better mindset to walk into events with.

Invest the time. It will take you more time to execute this strategy but it's totally worth it. In time you may pull back a little bit, as you become more successful, you have to become more selective about where we go. In the early days, just turn up. Go wherever you possibly can, and wherever you can find, because it's important to strengthen that relationship building muscle.

Networking is going to build the amount of people that know about you. It is going to build your online connections. You will start building a community and tribe of people that will resonate with who you are and what you do. You will build your confidence, you will clarify your message, even though as you're doing it you may feel really wonky.

Networking to this day, after 1000 days getting to a 7-figure business is the core way I market my business. I do get a lot of business online now, in fact 90% of our business comes from social media. Those social media connections have come from some face-to-face meetings, months or years prior.

Be patient. Oftentimes people will go to an event 3 or 4 times and say it is not working. I've found that it takes 7 to 8 months for a group of people to get to know you, and to start referring you. Patience is the most powerful way to build your business and if you're a local business it will work even more powerfully. This is because people like to know with whom they are doing business with and in the start up days you are more likely to have a reach just in the local area before it starts expanding wider and the word of mouth working more powerfully for you.

When I travel interstate, I look out for events where I can potentially visit and meet people. That physical contact works more powerfully than through words on an online network where they may see my name. I'm a big believer that this is the one thing that you must do whatever business you are in.

The networks that you attend will change. Research the networks you choose to attend to ensure they have people that are your cream target market or they advise your target market. Recently, through my authoring business, Ultimate 48-Hour Author, I realised that a great place to network was at the National Speakers Association of Australia.

I went there for four months in a row, and each month I came home with someone who wanted to do my authoring retreat. Why is that? Because, speakers, who are the core people who go to this particular association event all want to write books. The way we teach writing books is by speaking them out.

This is the ideal way for them to execute their books as well, so it is a perfect match. Within four months of being a member, I was asked to present the whole evening of speaking events and demo a book unpack. It was the biggest, most wonderful opportunity I got to be a part of and I could not believe that it happened so quickly.

Test and trial and then decide where you are going to invest your time and money when it comes to networking. Where does your cream market hang out? Ask yourself that question and then ask people around you. If you can't find a networking event, go on any forums or groups within your city that are being run by locals.

One of the things some business owners tell me is that they can't find any events. I simply say just ask around. After a while you are going to have to become selective, because there'll be so many choices of events.

Now is the time to commit to your top three actions that you are going to implement into your business as a result of reading this chapter. Here is some space for you to do that. Write it down, commit and make it part of the consistent actions that you will be taking to your 1000 days to a million-dollar coaching business from home.

3 Actions I Commit to Taking to Create my Million Dollar Business		
		Done ✔
1		
2		
3		

Gift Resource to assist in your Development from reading this Chapter: Develop your Barbeque Speech for Networking Success as part of the Ultimate Million Dollar Coaching Business from Home Workbook available to download at: https://natasadenman.leadpages.net/milliondollarcoach/ or by scanning this QR Code with your phone.

Chapter 3

Message

"You can't be everything to everyone but you can be something to someone."
– Drew Davis

The Americans have a famous saying: "The riches are the niches" and it's 100% true. Earlier in the journey of becoming a coach, a lot of coaches start out as generalists, but there's a certain point in time where niching is a must if you are to make it to a successful 6-figure and eventually 7-figure business. It is okay to be a generalist when you are starting out. I was a generalist for approximately the first 5–6 months.

With the help of my mentor, I started noticing what I was attracting and the types of problems that were coming to me so I could get more specific. Did I get specific? Oh, no. After the first 13 months, I actually continued chopping and changing and trialing different niches. I actually like to say that I dated a few different niches. I'll tell you a little bit about my story in niching later on.

Why is it so important to have a specific message and to appeal to a specific target market? It's crucial to be speaking to a particular person when you are offering a service. You cannot be everything to everyone, and the recipe for leverage and being an expert is hidden behind becoming a specialist in a specific area. After all, who makes more money, the general practitioner or the specialist?

You can charge a lot more and there is a lot less competition with what you're doing. You attract only those who want exactly what you have. It is much easier to market, grow the business and eventually scale it. The most important thing is, people who you meet out and about networking and online really know how and who to refer to you. It becomes a lot easier because everyone knows what you stand for.

There are people like the bucket list guy – he specialises in taking people away on retreats to create their bucket lists and then work on executing them. There are many other different people who are known for specific areas around branding, publicity or social media. They are known for that specific expertise within an area and use it as a lead into their sales funnels. Do they offer more than just their specialty? Most likely yes, but their marketing revolves purely around their hook.

What does it mean to have a specific message or niche as a coach? It means that you have a solution to a specific problem for a particular market that is willing to pay to have that problem solved. There is no point in niching as a coach in an area where people cannot or are not willing to spend the money to have their problem solved.

Let's go through my story on how I arrived at the niches that I have developed different business brands around. Initially, I was attracting a lot of people who wanted to work on their health. I ran this campaign where I got a lot of leads coming through for a weight loss coaching session. Everyone who was coming to me wanted specifically to lose 10 kilos.

My mentor at that time noticed this particular pattern as I described to him what these prospects were coming to me for, so he said to me: 'Natasa why don't you actually specialise in being the "Lose the Last 10 Kilos" girl?'

I thought about that and felt it was a pretty cool distinction because weight loss is so broad and there are so many solutions out there that blend into each other. If I could get really specific to that particular person who wants to lose the last 10 kilos, then that would make me different than everyone else. When my very first book came out, *The 7 Ultimate Secrets to Weight Loss*, I very soon rebranded.

My original brand was PRS Coaching (very generalist), and by rebranding to Ultimate Weight Loss, I aligned it with my book The 7 Ultimate Secrets to Weight Loss and added a tagline at the bottom of that branding – Lose the Last 10 Kilos. With those two components changed, my branding and the launch of my first book, it was the difference that made the difference. Within 90 days of that book release and the rebranding, I had a fully booked coaching practice with clients who understood exactly what I stood for and had what solution I was providing for a specific and measurable problem.

They really identified themselves within the tagline in what I was specialising regarding their weight-loss journey. This was the first step that got me to 6-figures within the first 500 days. Eventually, as I worked on the weight-loss niche, I created a program, I ran some online webinars, I recorded those, and also created a manual with a workbook and CDs that people could purchase, and have a do-it-yourself program for home.

A few short months later, I started attracting clients who were curious about how I had written a book. How had I created this program manual, and what was I doing to bring it into the market place? I started noticing that I was doing a lot more business mentoring around product development with people in the health and wellness industry. I really liked that the weight-loss niche was chugging along so nicely, but what I was really passionate about was business.

Very soon I realised that the weight-loss niche was my vehicle to get me to do the business mentoring. I went back to my mentor and said to him that I now wanted to focus more on helping business owners create what I had created. Had I not had that success within the weight-loss niche, there was no way that I could help practitioners and people in health and wellness build their businesses.

One thing you have to remember is that if you would like to be a business coach, you need to have succeeded in your own business. I really could not do business coaching when I initially started out as a coach. Once I built the weight-loss business, I had the score on the board and the proof in the pudding to actually position myself as a business mentor for people in health and wellness.

My mentor asked if I wanted to help businesses and how, specifically. For months we went back and forth around what kind of a tagline I would have to position my hook. I was saying things like start-up business coaching, women in business, solopreneurs – all quite generalist areas around business. Life coaching and business coaching on their own are both general and broad areas.

When we are talking about business coaching or business mentoring, how specifically was I going to position myself as a business mentor? Why was I any different from anyone else who represented themselves as a business coach? After all there are 1000's of business coaches out there. One night, as I was falling asleep, it came to me. It was right in front of my face. People kept coming to me about the product development. I brainstormed a few taglines, and ended up going with –Ultimate Business Edge – Create Products for Profit.

When I went back to my mentor, he said, 'You've got it, it's perfect. You have got your niche now around product and intellectual property development.' When I took that out into my networking that I did, created the brand of Ultimate Business Edge – Create Products for Profit, that was what made the difference and in turn I have so many people who were curious to talk to me about that, especially when I had shown the products that I had created for myself in my other business.

Within this brand I was mostly helping people that had businesses in health and wellness: practitioners, coaches, chiropractors, nutritionists. This was relevant to the industry that I had come from. Eventually, as time went on, I got even more specific within product development with the idea and creation of the Ultimate 48-Hour Author System, which is the way I'm writing this book. It is only going to take me 10 hours of speaking, at the most, and some time where I have unpacked these chapters to bring them to reality.

It is very important to start noticing what people see in you that they want for themselves, because that is the gold that you have that you can bring and create a system around. The system does not need to be complicated. The best systems are actually really simple and easy to understand and execute.

I want to help you find out, exactly how you can niche. There are a few questions to ask yourself and a few tips you can use to arrive at a specific niche that is going to really scream out to your ideal target market.

1. What do others see in you that they want for themselves? Really think about this one, because that is the thing that you can reverse engineer and work out a system around that you can bring out and sell to them as a solution.

2. What are you good at? Are you a great cook? Are you a very organised super-mum? Are you really good with your fitness routine? Are you fantastic at social media? Are you fantastic at generating publicity? What is it that you are good at?

3. Where have you spent your 10,000 hours? Wherever you have spent your 10,000 hours, you can comfortably call yourself an expert within that particular area. Often people try to separate their previous life to their life as coach, consultant or a mentor. However, everything that you have done, leading up to this point in life is relevant.

When I worked in the optical industry for 12 years managing stores from $250,000 turnover to $5 million dollars turnover when I left, I truly believe that those skills that I learnt there around building up the businesses to extraordinary levels, managing people, understanding the numbers, the profit and loss reports, creating systems for the stores that I used to run, all of those skills have been transferred into my business, and this is why a lot of people also see me as a super-organised person, who really knows exactly what is going on in her business.

4. Have flexibility to change, because you will most likely evolve into other niches from what you originally start doing as a coach. I started off in the health and wellness arena as a weight-loss coach to help people lose the last 10 kilos. However, to get to my purpose and my real passion which is helping business owners with their marketing, building products, credibility and expertise, I had to go through those first steps to show I have done it and to dissect the system in order to coach them through it.

5. Be different in a common niche. Ask yourself the question: How can I actually dissect this even further, so that it becomes quite unique to what I stand for and easy for people to remember?

6. Read books to get better and more knowledgeable. Follow what others are doing. Model what you like and pick up different things from different areas and people. Use your own expertise and then develop a model that you can bring out into the market. Nowadays nothing is new. Everything is repackaged and made sexy.

7. Ensure there is money in this niche. There is no point in creating products and programs for kids, teenagers and stay-at-home mums because they generally do not have the cash flow to be able to pay you. It is a great area that is close to many people's hearts, but you have to look after yourself before you can help others. Pick a niche that is going to generate cash flow, so that once you have that and your core life expenses are covered, you can then go out and help those kids, teenagers, and stay-at-home mums at cheaper or pro-bono rates.

8. Don't overthink it, just do something. Don't wait for clarity as I hear many people say. In the doing is where clarity comes from. As you are networking and saying what you do, this is where your clarity will come from.

One thing leads to another like getting my mentor from the first step and then going out and speaking to people and just developing relationships and externalising what I was doing got me to the clarity of what I stood for and whom I helped in the first 365 days.

Lastly, test out while you're networking what you have brainstormed at home and start noticing people's reactions to what you do. If you see curious looks on people's faces or them putting their hand up saying, that's me, you're talking about me, that's the problem that I have, then you're onto a good thing. If you see a lot of glazed eyes and no one asks questions, or shows curiosity after you have spoken, then perhaps, go back to the drawing board. If you get stuck and you just have absolutely no idea, you know what I'm going to say here again, go get a mentor and get them to help you develop your idea and niche. Even if you get someone who is going to help you for a couple of hours to really ask you the right questions and give you an expert view on what you should go and specialise in.

If you have chosen a niche, and it's not working, then I'm going to tell you the same thing my first mentor told me – don't be too precious about anything. Adjust and be flexible. Sometimes you do not need to change the content that you have developed and created around that particular niche, all you need to do is just change the message and the branding around it and test it out with the new make-up.

As I said, nothing nowadays is brand new. Everything is repackaged and made to seem brand new. For example, one of Tony Robbins' mentors was Jim Rohn. Some of the concepts and ideas that he speaks about, he learnt from Jim Rohn and I can guarantee Jim Rohn learnt them from someone else before him. I have learnt those same ideas and concepts from Tony Robbins, who has been one of my mentors.

Realistically, there are no secrets. Ideas and products are repackaged so that they apply to today's world, society and markets so that it's sexy and attractive and people are driven to invest so they can help themselves and the coach can facilitate the process.

The last thing that may be an issue for you is that you may not be a person who's driven by money. I hear that a lot. You want to help people like teenagers, kids or stay-at-home parents. If you can't sustain your life financially, you have to work and if you are working 40 hours per week, how many can you possibly help in a niche where people cannot pay you? I suggest developing a niche in a lucrative area, then using the funds to help yourself and those who can't afford your services but are close to your heart.

We have arrived at that part of the chapter where you take responsibility and give yourself three actions and tasks that you will complete as a result of what you have just read. Use the space below to put those actions in there and get to work. In this particular chapter, you may like to answer some of the key questions that'll help you arrive at your profitable, lucrative niche. All the best!

3 Actions I Commit to Taking to Create my Million Dollar Business		
		Done ✔
1		
2		
3		

Gift Resource to assist in your Development from reading this Chapter: Discover your Avatar (ideal client) Questionnaire as part of the Ultimate Million Dollar Coaching Business from Home Workbook available to download at: https://natasadenman.leadpages.net/milliondollarcoach/ or by scanning this QR Code with your phone.

Chapter 4
Support

"Good teams become great ones, when the members trust each other enough to surrender the 'me' for the 'we'."
– Phil Jackson

Families that grow together, stay together. Couldn't be truer. Thinking back when I started my business, my husband was very much in an employee type of mindset. He'd go to work, come home, make dinner for us, which was so fantastic, and then spend the rest of the evening watching TV. It was the same thing the next day, and the next day, and the next day, until the weekend came. I was totally immersed in the business and there was a real disconnect between us in the beginning.

As time went on, he started to notice a lot of changes in me and realised that he should perhaps start reading some of the books that I was reading and getting involved in some of the things that I was doing. As we started to diverge, there came a time where we both realised that if we kept diverging we wouldn't end up being together for much longer.

He decided to start converging in my direction, as he could see the positive changes that I was making and how much happier I was with the things that I was doing. Truly living my passion and purpose in what I was put on this earth to do. His day job was not his passion and purpose, therefore, he was also looking for a way out.

Family is so important as they provide that encouragement in the tough times. As you build the business, there will be a lot more tough times to begin with, especially in the first couple of years. There is a lot of support that you need when it comes to building a business, which is available all around you if you are willing to be helped.

I wanted to outsource the cleaning of my house early on. I did that for a few weeks but it wasn't sustainable because financially we could not afford to have a cleaner then. Nowadays, we do but back then it was just not something that could be fitted into the budget, especially if I wanted to pay for my mentoring and the programs that I was undertaking to learn how to build the business faster and smarter.

Family gives us a sense of belonging because when we are new in business, we feel like a duck out of the pond. By coming home and having that support, it keeps us in a place where we feel there is familiarity, which is very important to us as human beings. Also, consider the financial support. The financial support when the business is in the red that's provided perhaps by that partner, who is still in a day job, is crucial so that we can focus on building the business.

This is why I always encourage people to remain in their day jobs or downsize to part-time work, so they can have a sustainable way to keep the business going. No matter what, at the end of the day, your family will love you. Focus and remember that. Know that you have their support, even though sometimes they may be skeptical or keep quiet in the corner.

What kind of support would you look for from your family? I've broken it down to three different types of support: physical, financial and emotional. The key to all of these three is communication. It is the crucial ingredient to success, as others can seem to feel left out, ignored, taken advantage of and maybe a little resentful around what you're doing.

Sometimes our families may think that we're being self-centered because we've decided to go down this path and all we can talk about is different business strategies that we're going to implement, Communication is truly crucial and getting people involved in what you're doing will make them feel a lot more at ease around your big vision to achieve your 7-figure business.

Let's talk about the three different levels of support. I will not assume that you have a partner to support you or a mum that can take care of the children. We'll look at some other ways that you can achieve the same outcome and continue building your business.

The physical support on my journey was the support around the house;

upkeep, cooking and shopping, and all of those things that go into maintaining an orderly household. The second part was the babysitting support because I had one child when I started my business and soon after I had my second baby. I am now days from having my third. This support was huge and it wasn't always available, so I kept up a juggling act around the kids. I found a childcare center that would take in my kids on a casual basis. Each and every week I would give them the days that I would want them to be looked after. I had a friend who lived around the corner, who also didn't mind babysitting if I had to go out to a networking event. She helped me a lot since Stuart and my mum worked full time.

At the same time, in my first 300 days of business, I remained in my part-time job and worked 3 days a week. I worked Sunday, Monday, and a 12-hour Thursday, which is how I was covering my core expenses around my education within my business. My husband's wages were covering the core bills at home, the food and the bare necessities we needed to survive.

Babysitting was hard to come by. I felt like I was begging, borrowing and stealing time from people. I'm truly grateful for the opportunities that they enabled me to have in terms of connecting with fellow business owners. I mixed it up between my father-in-law, my mum who was always up for babysitting on the weekend, that friend of mine and the casual childcare centre.

I used different strategies to get support. The housework and upkeep was my husband's forte as he has always been a very nurturing person who does all the cooking for the family too. I am very blessed that way. He undertook those duties that then enabled me to continue working in the business and on the business until the very late hours of the night and also on weekends.

Think about yourself. How can you utilise different avenues of support when it comes to running your business? You will need to go out and connect with people as we've spoken about before. If you're a single parent and have no family to support you, perhaps look at asking for help from friends or other parents in business who you can do swaps with.

When you go out networking, you will meet other parents in business who are also single parents. Could you work out a roster of how you could help one another out to take care of the kids when you have to do other business activities? There is certainly always a way and as the famous saying goes – where there's a will, there's always a way. If it's important to you, you will find a way and if it's not, you will find an excuse.

Think about it in a way that the sacrifices that you're making around being able to get out there and build that foundation of your business will be rewarded in due course. You will be able to provide your children with financial abundance and the things that you cannot right now. For example, spending quality time doing awesome things because you have choice, going on the holidays you have always wanted, buying the luxuries you have always skimped on and enjoying the month over the festive season doing and having whatever your heart desires.

The second type of support is financial. This kind of support is crucial to get right, because so many people and business owners end up playing the ignorant card when it comes to finances. They are unaware of what's going in or what's going out. Basically, they're not aware of whether they're living above their means or below their means, even before they start out in business.

The one thing that I have always done for myself since I first moved out of home at the age of 20, is a household budget in terms of what's coming in every week and what's going out every week. A very basic spreadsheet that tells me how much I have got to play with. I need to know where I need to cut down so I don't go deeper into debt.

I have always been the type of person who pays off the credit card each and every week, depending on what I have spent on it. My rule is to only have one to look after and to never let it go in excess of one to two thousand dollars, depending on the time of the year. Looking after core financials is crucial and understanding your core financials is one of the essential ingredients if you are going to create your business to be 6-figures and beyond.

Involve your partner to help you and make decisions together on the investments to build the business because as you make more money in your business, you will also find that you will need to spend more money. If you want to build your business to the very next level then you will need to reinvest in it to get you there.

The more you grow, the more professional and bigger you brand will become and you will want to bring out different qualities and a more professional look. In the early days, most things are DIY – I was doing videos myself. However, recently, I have been hiring a professional videographer to do some promotional and sales videos on my behalf. This way I come across as more established, professional and sharp with my branding and the asking price of my products and services reflects the quality of work that I deliver.

Just because you may be making a lot more money doesn't mean that the profit is larger. It means that you will be outsourcing and continuing to invest a lot more to bring in more leads and prospects so that your business scales to 7 figures.

The last type of support is emotional support. This is so important early on in the business because we can be hard on ourselves and often get feelings of not being good enough to experience success. A lot of new business owner's crumble after being rejected time after time. The amount of no's that you are going to get early on in business are going to be much more than later on. Your conversion rate will change as you change and become more confident in speaking out about what you do and how you deliver it.

The feelings of failure and rejection are more likely to turn up a lot more in the early days. By having emotional support from your family you will be able to overcome mindset setbacks that you experience. There are lows in business and there will be peaks and troughs at every stage. Tough times don't last, tough people do. Your family is there to believe in you and to remind you of how tough you are.

Throughout my years of being in business, I have realised that there come moments where you can have a sense of losing your business or there's not going to be a business in a few months.

Your family is there to listen, to hear you concerns, as well as to celebrate successes with you. If your partner can't see your vision and is skeptical about what you're doing, my biggest advice would be to practice patience in the early days with him/her. As I said earlier in this chapter, my husband Stuart kept living the same kind of day over and over for the first 12 to 18 months. What I know now is that when you prove yourself and you can show that your hard work is paying off, they will come around and join your tribe. Show that you are a hard worker. Don't waste time and money because you will have them on board before you know it.

They will see that you're doing the best you can with what you've got, and that will prevail as long as you persist. In no situation, where someone has truly given their hardest and removed the excuses and the BS out of the way, has someone not been able to get to results. I can guarantee you that.

Other people that you may feel a lack of support from when you start out as a business owner can be a lot of your old friends and groups that you used to hang out with. You may find that they just don't get it and that's okay. In this situation, unfortunately, or maybe fortunately, your circle of friends is likely to change because of the shift in your values. You may have valued a social life a lot higher in the past and now you're valuing your business and creating that wealth and security for your family. A stay-at-home mum versus an employee versus a business owner all have different types of mindsets. None are good or bad, they are just different.

Remember that soon you will make new friends and have amazing relationships with them. When you have similar values, the relationship-building phase happens a lot quicker because you have things in common to talk about. You might need to let go of the old world and be alone for a little while, and then enter the new world where those new exciting challenges and people await you and really stretch you to reach new levels of growth and progress.

There is a famous saying, 'You are who you're with, or you become the person from the average of the top 5 people you hang out with'. Look at the five people you hang out with the most and ask yourself whether that is where you want to see yourself in five to ten years time? The result will be that that is exactly what will unfold.

Having Fun in Business

You started your business so you can live life on your terms and serve people in a way that is fulfilling and doesn't feel like work. What tends to happen with new business owners, I have observed, is that they get really focused while they're out there completing their to-do lists, planning their goals, and doing all the hard work that it takes to build that business. After reaching a point close to burnout a year or two later, they realise that this is not what they signed up for. Building a business is a lot harder than having a job.

They decide to go back to a job and they go back to the real world – to the old world. One of the sayings that I learnt at a training I was at with my husband in my first year of business, was, 'This is simple, This is easy, oh my God, This if fun!'

When I'm doing things that are difficult and unfamiliar, which is most of the things you'll be doing in the first one to two years, it's really important to say this particular line at the top of your voice because what it does is embed the fact that it's simple, easy, and fun. At the same time, it may not be and couldn't be further from the truth. That saying is something that we use at our Ultimate 48-Hour Author Weekends because what we are doing is not simple, easy, or fun. We kept embedding that because it helps make your words become a reality.

Another thing I used to love doing and still do is rewarding myself and executing my rewards regularly. It's one thing to say you will reward yourself and another to see it through. Business owners often feel that rewards can only happen when they are making lots of money and they don't deserve it any earlier. They wait and wait until there isn't much to look forward to and they become a slave to their business.

In the first 12 months, for every client I would sign up I would have a reward pre-planned. Sometimes it was a monetary reward and other times it was non-monetary, but I'd always have something very little that I would be able to claim upon signing up a client.

Take your family away, reward them all, spend time together and have fun, because when you do that, you move away from the focused life of business and you will bring back the fun. You will also bring back the creativity, which will allow you to then develop new programs, products and approaches within your business that will make it more abundant.

Success in business is based on focus and creativity. What I normally tell people is that creativity does not occur if you're constantly being focused Monday through to Sunday because it's not going to develop and grow as quickly as possible. That is why I normally work Monday to Thursday and have Friday to Sunday off to let my creativity flow. This many not be feasible early on. Give yourself at least 24 hours each week for creative time until you can give yourself more.

Focused time is your Monday to Thursday. Your creativity time is a spontaneous time where you have nothing scheduled in your diary. This is why I often take my family on long weekends away at least once a month.

We go on a couple of big holidays overseas or somewhere we can be totally be away from the focused space that we have while we are executing things around our business.

Creativity occurs when there is spontaneity. Use that and bring it back into your world even if in the beginning you must be focused for 90% of the time. At least allow yourself half a day or a day where you can let your mind wander. Just yesterday, I was reading a post on what successful people do. In this particular post your most creative time is in the evening before you go to bed.

Some of you may say – I'm a morning person, that's when I'm most productive, but we're not talking here about productivity. We're talking about creativity. Why is it that we are most creative at night? Because you are tired towards the end of the day. When you're tired, what happens is, you let go of the focus you needed throughout the day, and you're able to just let your mind wander. If you want access to some creative time why not spend half an hour or an hour to do that of the evening. I have been doing this most nights without knowing it. And when I read it yesterday, I thought, wow, that is really cool.

Value fun as the business can consume your life. It's unfortunate if it does as oftentimes that is what makes it unsustainable.

You must be able to keep your enthusiasm and optimism high if you want to have a sustainable business. Part of that is having fun with it. That's why one of my highest values is fun. I always say if it's fun I'll do it and execute it. Not everything I do in the business is fun. Not everything you will do with me fun, because if it is you don't have a business, you have a hobby. Hobbies cost you money, they don't make you money.

Now that you have read this chapter, it is your turn. Sit down and write three things that you will start doing as a result of what I have shared with you. This was an important and crucial part of getting to the success that

I have achieved over the past 1000 days. And I would not take it back for a second.

Would I do things differently if I had my time again? Maybe I would involve my husband a lot more into the business in the early days, so that we didn't feel the disconnect that we felt. I take everything as feedback and there's a learning experience in all that I have been through now being on the other side of the coin I can bring it back to you and explain how it was, what happened and how we made it work. You get to choose your course of action from my experiences.

3 Actions I Commit to Taking to Create my Million Dollar Business		
		Done ✔
1		
2		
3		

Gift Resource to assist in your Development from reading this Chapter: 'Where am I financially Budget Spreadsheet' as part of the Ultimate Million Dollar Coaching Business from Home Workbook available to download at: https://natasadenman.leadpages.net/milliondollarcoach/ or by scanning this QR Code with your phone.

Chapter 5
People

"People do business with people because they choose to, not because they have to. We can always find others doing the same thing or selling the same product, it's the personal connection that makes the difference."
– Unknown

People buy people. I would love for you to take this as truth when dealing with potential clients in a business. It doesn't matter if you're selling hardware, software or coaching, at the end of the day, if people like you, trust you, and believe that you will look after them and keep them safe, they will buy you.

And as a coach people buy what you have created for yourself. They invest emotionally in the results that you have and the person that you have become before they consider what it is you're selling and how you actually deliver it.

It is very important to remember that you are the person that your client wants to become. It is what's within you that they want for themselves. This is what we discussed in the niching chapter around your message and it becomes relevant here again. This chapter is very much about investing that time to build amazing relationships with people. Why would you want to do that? Word of mouth is huge when it comes to being a coach. Often it can sustain your whole business without any need for paid advertising.

Getting referrals from people is a surefire way that you will convert those referrals and word of mouth recommendations into clients a lot easier. By building relationships with people, you build new friendships and you start to get that sense of belonging to a specific group. You will start to get that support that you wouldn't get elsewhere, especially not from your old world. There's that trust, intimacy and sharing that occurs with people who are in business and striving for similar goals. Understand that success is not a solo act early on and you will build an amazing enterprise in time.

Coaching is all about people IQ. Coaches are master rapport builders. We assist others in making the changes for themselves to create those new worlds that they want to belong to. At the end of the day, whom you hang out with will transform who you also become. Dr Steve Maraboli said, 'If you hang out with chickens, you're going to cluck. If you hang out with eagles, you're going to fly.' Think about who you're hanging out with and how that will project in your life and in the business you are creating.

If you don't focus on building relationships, I can guarantee you that your success and sales will be a lot less and they will take a lot longer to generate. Trying to do it all alone on this journey only guarantees you will take 10 times longer to get there, because you're not accessing the people around you to help and support you with their expertise.

Is there a difference between professional and personal relationships? What do you think? I believe they're much of the same thing because originally you may meet someone at a business networking event and act in a very professional manner. As time progresses you see this person time and time again, and as this happens they get more involved and knowledgeable of your personal life. This is why when I use social media, I don't really separate my professional and personal profiles because I want people to see all of me not just parts of me. I have nothing to hide and am honest and integral about everything I do.

As a coach, it is very important that people know you on that personal level because your future clients are buying who you have become and who you are being. If you are not displaying a side of you that is humanized and a side of you that people want to have access to and want to become themselves, then you will have less of an ability to sell the programs and products that you have. Ultimately, as a coach, people are buying some part of your life that you have created and are living for yourself.

After all, why are you reading this book? You are reading this book because you want to get inside my head. You want to get inside how I think, what

I've done, how I do it, so that you can model those actions, strategies and tools that I share with you to some extent to get the results that I have achieved in the last 1000 days. I don't blame you because I do the same. I have role models in my life who I follow and watch what they do and I'm curious how they got there, and what was their defining moment or turning point that made it all possible to achieve success.

In my business you will have noticed as you're reading this book, I keep going back to relationships. The core approach that I believe has been the key to my success is to nurture, connect and leverage my relationships and at the same time have lots of fun with the people that I'm meeting and generating lots of real-life conversations that result eventually in sales.

Sometimes people are unsure how to approach relationship-building and it doesn't come naturally to everyone. Some are not good at maintaining a relationship. I always say, keep the ball in your court and if people don't want to keep in touch with you, don't take things personally because it's never about you. It's very rarely about you. If you hear it down the line, take it on board as feedback. Nurturing and staying in touch with people is very important. This is why I always take the initiative myself to connect and start a conversation. If the other person responds fantastic, but remember this – 8 out of 10 people will not respond so move on and keep connecting.

In the time that I have been out and about meeting people, I can only count on my two hands how many people have actually sent up a follow-up email or connected with me on social media and even less picked up the phone to ring me. It's okay being different, because if it were easy to build and nurture relationships, everyone would be doing it. They are not doing it. One of the other things that I always say is if you're not doing it, you don't know it even if you have learnt it before. This is called information gathering. When you're doing it, you do know it and what it actually takes and that's called experience.

Having systems around maintaining your relationships is what will bring you business, never-ending prospects, leads, clients and financial security. One of the biggest things that I also do is respond very quickly to any enquiries or requests not just from prospects but all of my clients. Most of the time, it's under 24 hours. At worst, it would be 48 hours if it is the weekend. We live in a very fast-paced world that wants answers promptly, so responding quickly to people's enquiries is crucial to building your business rapidly.

When people are hot and heavy for you, you want to get to the point where they can make a decision with all the information that you have shared with them. If they see you respond quickly, they know that when you look after them they will get the same type of service. And please don't pretend to be responding quickly at the sign up stage and then let go of that when working with someone. That is really bad customer service and I have been at the other end of it a few times myself, which is really disheartening.

I have come across business owners who have been very keen, very responsive, until they got the business. Then you're chasing them up and trying to get some communication happening to no avail. Please don't be one of those business owners. There's nothing worse than promising one thing and then delivering another, especially when someone has invested with you.

Use those relationships that you have built already to ask for help. Offer people you know to help them with your expertise. The universe works in funny ways. You may not get it back from that person but you will get it from somewhere else. Going in with the attitude of givers gain, and your gain will come so long as you help and give full heartedly. It always balances out at the end of the day.

There is no need to pitch others when you offer help because they will come to you from the results they see you help them achieve. My type of selling happens very organically. People like to call it selling without selling because my results actually sell what I do. My life, what I do, the actions I take is everything I live, breathe and teach. I will never teach anything that I have not done myself.

When I help others, they often bring up the question of how else can you help me? What else do you have that you can offer people like me? I then go into the sales conversation. Oftentimes it is not a formal sales meeting that I have because when I focus on relationships, the sales just happen. If this is your type of style and the way you would like to build a business, then follow the strategies and tools that I share.

There are different ways of selling. There is cold calling using heavily persuasive scripts, based on NLP principles. Then there is polarisation of people, which means sometimes making people feel inadequate in order for them to make a decision to work with you. Those strategies are successful so long as they feel good about the person using them.

They don't appeal to me, at the same time I'm okay that others use them because if they work with them that's all that matters. Some of the things that you may think about is that you may not be great at making new friends. To build a relationship, it takes time. It takes multiple touch points with people to create that closeness.

My suggestion is to take part in social events rather than business networking events to build your relationships. Have social events with your business buddies because sometimes you see people in a business networking event and they're a certain person and may be putting on that professional face, but other times you go out for a round of bowling or some group team activity and you see them in a whole different light.

It's really great to mix up the types of events that you go to with people to create that closer bond. It does take time to keep in touch with people. I always say it's time well invested. Bank your relationships because they may not turn into sales today or tomorrow or even 3 or 6 months down the track. I always have a little smirk, a laugh and I smile to myself when people have followed me and have stayed in touch, have asked for small bits of help along the way and then 18 months–2 years later, they come and say, 'Hey Nat, I really want to do this program with you. I want you to mentor me or I want to come into this particular group coaching style that you have.'

I love when that happens because I know that it's been worthwhile that whole time that I have kept in touch. I have to say though, I don't keep in touch because I know in 18 months or 2 years people will come to work with me. Some of them do and some of them don't, I treat everyone the same, I am genuinely interested in people and helping them and the beauty is, if that person doesn't end up working with me, they usually will refer someone else because they know and trust me.

There is something that comes back to me when I go to events and that is how people have heard about me from other people. So many times I have turned up at an event and someone has said: 'Oh, I heard someone talk about you yesterday and I've now run into you at this event.' That's usually the common comment that gets made. I find that very amusing and flattering that others are talking about me, which means that my message and my personality has provoked someone to say something about the brand, what we offer and how we do it. I then have instant credibility, instant trust and intimacy with that person because we also know someone else in common.

One of the biggest reasons why businesses fail is due to failure of follow-up, response and nurturing. 97% of people will not do due diligence and have systems in place to follow up their relationships. Live in the 3%. Set up your structure and process of follow up. This will make your life easier, more automated and result is a super successful business.

Focus on those people who do want to develop relationships and leverage those strong bonds that you create over a period of time. I can guarantee you, when you make relationships the key focus, and you practice patience with them, you will get to the success you desire and deserve. Recently we were connected with a very influential business owner in Australia, who is not even a local to our home city of Melbourne. It's been awesome to get to know him and to help each other out.

We started that relationship 4–5 months ago with my husband and he have continued to develop that relationship with this particular person. We're not in it to leverage anything at this point in time; we're just getting to know each other. We are getting a sense of what they are like, what we are like, what our values are and whether they are aligned because not all the time that you meet someone is going to align with your values.

Values are very important in relationships. What I have found is that one of my highest values is doing things at a very speedy rate. I have always been that quick responsive person and if the other person is not like that when I'm creating a joint venture or strategic alliance with them, it's not going to go off well because I will end up being frustrated. That's exactly what has happened in some of the relationships that I thought started off with the similar set of values, but ended up being quite different from each other.

I trust that this chapter has given you a lot of food for thought when it comes to how much time and effort you should invest in your relationships. They will make or break your business. Write down the three things that you will do to nurture those relationships in your life and build new ones towards the success that you deserve.

3 Actions I Commit to Taking to Create my Million Dollar Business		
		Done ✔
1		
2		
3		

Gift Resource to assist in your Development from reading this Chapter: 'Relationship Building Checklist System' as part of the Ultimate Million Dollar Coaching Business from Home Workbook available to download at: https://natasadenman.leadpages.net/milliondollarcoach/ or by scanning this QR Code with your phone.

Chapter 6
Expert

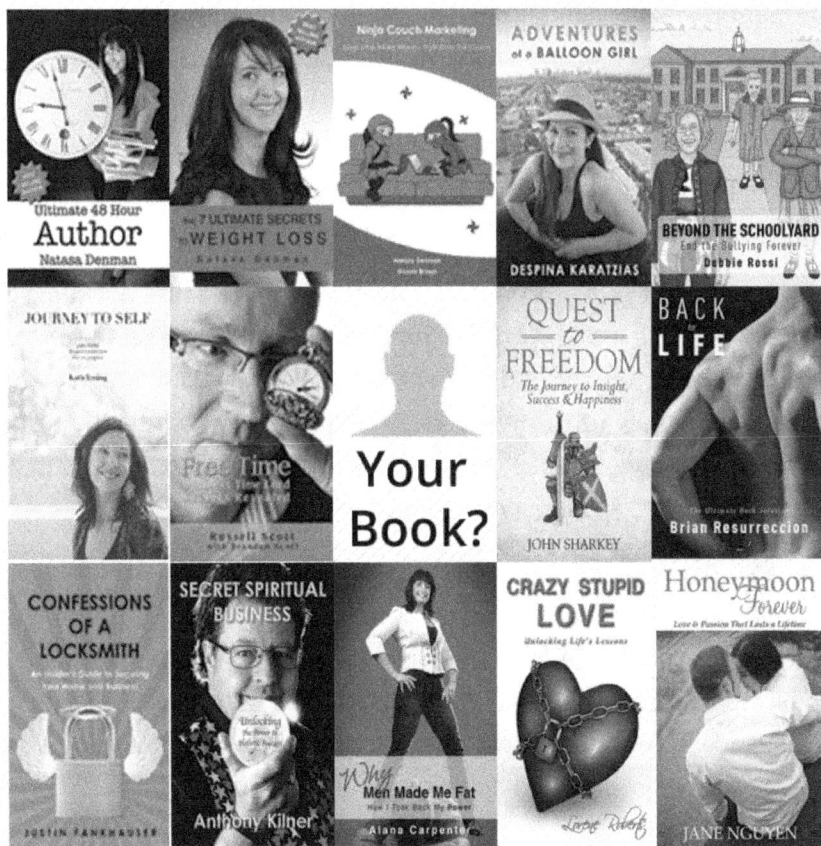

"By publishing content that shows buyers you understand their problems and can show them how to solve them, you build credibility."
– Ardath Albee

Thus far we have looked at the intangible ways of how I built my business and the steps that I took in the first 6 months, which have remained consistent over the past 1000 days. It is now time to look at some of the tangible products that really propelled me to create fantastic cash flow and abundance so that the business becomes viable.

Six months into my journey I had a coffee meeting with a person that I met at a networking event. He saw how I was passionate about helping people and after hearing the stuff I knew and loved about human behaviour he said to me, 'Nat, you should write a book! You know a lot about your expertise, you can pull all this together in a book. A book is the best business card that you can possibly have and great for your marketing.'

Well don't give me a half decent idea because if I think it's got some legs, I'll definitely take it on board. Not even 4–5 weeks later, I set a New Year's goal to write my very first book over the following 90 days. Writing my first book was unknown territory. I had no idea what I was getting myself into and how long it would take. Previous to writing it, I had attempted to write a book 4–5 times and stopped at about page 15–20.

I set a 90-day goal and I said that I want to write 90 pages. Break that down over 90 days, I asked myself, 'Who can't write a page a day?' I wasn't going to write just one page a day because once your thoughts flow through you'll want to continue. I planned instead to sit down twice a week for 2 hours and write 3–4 pages per sitting which would give me the 7–8 pages a week to keep me on track to my goal.

That's exactly what I did. I broke it down and consistently even when I wasn't inspired to write, I sat and wrote anyway. I got to those 90 pages in 80 days. Three months later the book was self-published and it was an incredible defining moment and the turnaround within my business.

Up until that point I had only 3 paying clients. I had only generated $7,000 of income in 400 days, which was so far in the red zone. I had already invested in lots of courses to learn how to build my coaching practice and by day 400 I certainly did not have a viable business or even a business that way in positive cash flow.

The following 90 days as the book got launched, my business grew from having 2–3 clients all up to 15–20 clients that I was coaching and mentoring around personal life coaching as well as the weight-loss coaching.

This is where we also rebranded from the old brand that didn't say very much from PRS Coaching to Ultimate Weight Loss – Lose the Last 10 Kilos.

Why would you want to become an author? You just read about the amazing opportunities that come from it. For me it was about positioning myself as an expert and being seen as someone that was professional and highly disciplined in what I wanted to achieve. It was to build further trust and intimacy with my ideal clients. Some of the comments I get when I work with people is that they tell their friends and colleagues that they're working with an author, which is very special for them.

Becoming an author as a coach or a small business owner opens up a lot of doors when it comes to publicity and speaking opportunities. You're more likely to be considered as a speaker at an event and get your articles into magazines and get on radio and TV when you are published.

The perception that people have of you when you're an author is also so different from not having anything to back up what you stand for. Just think about the perception people have of the car salesperson versus an author. Authors are considered to be disciplined, professional, knowledgeable, intelligent and nice people in general. That perception is big leverage when you want to build your business.

The beauty is that authoring is not just about the book. I'm a big believer that the book is only 25% of the journey and that the real leverage is in the fact that you can develop further programs and products from it. There is so much more potential in terms of your return on investment that you get through selling those rather then being focused on book sales. Ultimately for all the coaches reading this book, a book truly turns your intangible service-based business into a tangible product that is something that you can share with your clients.

It's really nice for people to walk away with your programs, manuals, workbooks etc. These are all of the things that you can develop from becoming an author from your intellectual property beyond writing the book alone.

There are opinions out there that you shouldn't be writing a book too soon into your business journey. With my story, I have proven that to be wrong. My belief is write the book first and then build the business from it and leverage and expand from it beyond that. Everyone will have a different opinion when and how you should write a book.

What you need to be mindful of is what the purpose is for your book. If you are going to focus on having a best-seller and thousands of books and book sales as your primary intention then writing it too early is going to be a mistake, because you wouldn't have the network or people following you to generate those sales. You must first build a name for yourself. If the purpose is to leverage and develop other products and programs, then certainly writing a book early on and creating the other intellectual property from it, is the way to go.

There are two reasons why people don't write a book and neither of those reasons are the common excuses that come up for people first up: time and/or money. Having spoken to my publisher and the amount of people I have now dealt with around writing a book, it turns out that fear and procrastination holds people back. The fear of standing out, being successful and speaking your truth is way bigger than fear of failure in my experience. People are scared of their own magnificence.

The fear I hear a lot is, 'Who am I to say that I'm the expert?' Or procrastination comes in the form of an excuse that it takes too long to write a book. Due to these big objections from people, I have developed the *Ultimate 48-hour Author Retreat Program.* I managed to nip procrastination in the bud and give people a system that makes it easy and simple. This way they could see how this can be leveraged in a bigger way beyond just the book. I often talk to them about the fact that you've had enough life experience and you know what you stand for, what you believe in. Write about that. Always remember that the books you end up writing are books to the old version of you. They are for your past self.

For example, I'm writing this 1000 days after I started my business and I'm writing it to what the Natasa Denman of 1000 days ago needed to know in order to get the results she has today. What steps she would need to execute and what to avoid now being at the other end of a goal achieved.

This is the way people do it. It was the same thing when I wrote the *Ultimate 48 Hour Author* book. That book was the system that I needed when I was writing my very first book, which took 90 days. Nowadays I can pull together a book with a few hours of preparation and speaking out the chapters on my expertise and knowledge.

So when should you write a book? Now. Start today! This is my fifth book and I learn and grow every year. What you know up until now is good enough. If you sat down to write in a month or two from now, you're most likely going to write something different. I say seize the moment and trust that you will come out with awesome information that someone will find value and gold nuggets in.

Same thing goes for this particular book. If I am to speak out this chapter in a few weeks time I probably may be saying something slightly different.

There is a famous saying out there for coaches and trainers – No training is ever the same, the content may be the same, the Power Point presentation that you might be using will the same, but the stories that get told, the questions that get asked and the things that pop into your mind as you're going through the delivery are different every single time.

Nothing is ever perfect – focus and use that 80/20 principle. Remember if you don't write a book, your credibility will stagnate and the opportunities around you will not be as abundant. The trust that you develop with people initially will take a lot longer to develop and that will mean it will be a lot harder for you to sell your other products and programs.

Really think about where you put importance when it comes to positioning yourself. Writing a book for a coach, mentor or a consultant is one of the key ingredients to generate that amazing business card that your personal brand stands for.

How do you go about writing a book? I have written a whole book on how to do it in 48 hours, so if you wanted a more detailed system pick up my *Ultimate 48 Hour Author* book and you'll get that whole system on how to execute yours in just 48 hours. Here I will share with you three brief steps on what's involved. It's really simple once you understand it.

1. Unpack your intellectual property. What I do with people is to brainstorm what the different steps are that they have taken to overcome a certain problem. As you can see from this book I am unfolding the steps on how I got to the million dollar coaching business at home and those steps are then put into the order of how things happened over that time frame.

The initial chapters were about the intangible side of things, the relationships the networking, the support of the family and as we're moving through we're starting to get through the actionable more tangible product creation, authoring and creating high-end programs as well as running events and speaking and publicity.

When unpacking intellectual property you don't need to have it in order at the beginning. Just sit down and see if you can come up with 12 different topics that you could then put in order to create the flow of structure and steps for your book. I have also created the *Ultimate Book Unpack Formula Video E-Course*, which is a series of 6 videos with some templates that you can get access to via a link that I will provide in the resources. If you want access to the videos email us to purchase the E-Course.

Once you have written out what your broad topics are, put them in order. We then need to convert them. What I mean by that is converting those topics into something a little bit sexier that sells people what they want and gives people what they need which we discussed in the messaging chapter of this book.

Use of hypnotic words and hypnotic language to make those topics in your book title really entice people to be curious enough to pick it up and start reading. This applies to your chapter names, to your book title overall and the blurb at the back of your book. Once you have put all of those things in order, I will supply you with a template that I use to unpack people's books and then unpack each chapter.

Unpacking each chapter means listing out what you want to write about. I use the format system. This means I cover off the *why*, the benefits of reading that chapter, which you read about earlier. I covered of what are the benefits of becoming an author? What are you going to talk about in that particular chapter? For example, here we are speaking about how you would go about writing a book and then we get into the nitty gritty of the *how*. This contains tips, tools and steps on getting you to execute the *what*. At the end of each chapter we go through the What Ifs. That means what are some objections that people would come up with after having read the content that you have written about.

I use this method when delivering webinars, workshops and speaking events. It truly is a neat way of pulling information together and really appealing to every type of personality. There are some people who are why people, others are what people, others just want the how and be given all the steps. And finally there are these people that are what if this and what if that type of people? They are the ones who want to throw the objections around. It is really valuable to be able to handle objections. Not just in workshops, but also within a book the reader is always judging the content and having questions arise in their mind.

This is where this system covers all of that and it gives people closure in terms of what you've said in each and every chapter. Last tip on how to get your book executed is to set a schedule. If you don't want to do it the way I'm doing it right now, by speaking it out you can also get it done the traditional way. Some of our authors who come to the retreats actually decide to sometimes type their books out. That's okay if that's their preference, but I'd say 80% end up speaking them out as its so much faster and easier and 20% type them. They also sometimes come to the retreat with a typed up manuscript to learn the leveraging components of how to use the book beyond its publishing.

If you are going to break it down and do it the traditional way be consistent. Set the dates, book in scheduled appointments with yourself in your diary so that you sit down in those moments and you treat them just like you would if you had a paying client booked in. That is what I did and as I said yes you'll hit roadblocks in terms of not having inspiration or thinking to write something that's insightful. It's okay, stick it out, it will pass and you will bring your book out in no time. Some days you will sit down and you will write 7–10 pages without blinking.

It's very important to have guidance in terms of the steps to take on how to self-publish. A lot of people don't start because they just haven't got that clarity around what those steps are. That's why with the *Ultimate 48 Hour Author Retreat Program* it's a fully done for you system. We have hired publishers and everyone is ready for your work to be handed in with us mentoring you along the way and giving you the steps of what to do next.

There are some common myths around authoring.

Let's handle some of your objections right now. One of the biggest ones is that people don't believe that they're an expert in a particular area. What I would like you to think about right here is what is an expert and why are they different from someone who is not? Is it the time they've spent within a certain industry, the time they've executed a certain talent or a skill. Certainly that may position them as an expert, but remember the information that you have, you are an expert in your life, you've spent 10s of thousands of hours with what you're doing and being a coach, consultant or a mentor, they're the experiences that people are investing in to have through what you are passionate about delivering. There is always someone in the world that needs what you've got to offer. Think about who you are failing to serve.

When I look back at my weight-loss book, I think it's almost like a primary school level for the *me* right now. However, I am still proud of that book because I still consistently get emails from people that tell me I've changed their life. They are consistently using it as a guide and a manual to go back to when they're having mindset challenges around their weight.

Australia is very multicultural and some people don't have English as their first language. The beauty of everything that we teach and how we teach is that everyone can write the book they want to write. As long as they know the system and how to execute those templates, we have had people who are from a Vietnamese background and Italian with very heavy accents still write their books in English. The feedback on their books has been that they are some of the best ones that we've ever done.

If you feel you have no information, think again. Once you go through the unpacking process, you will be able to dissect that information so that you do have enough to speak out a 30,000–40,000 word book. Everyone that I've worked with without fail has struggled in to cut back the information rather than to execute more of it.

The last thing that comes up is that there's a perception that publishing is only for the rich people or that it's quite expensive. But it doesn't have to be that way as there are certain publishing packages that can exist out there as options. We hire a self publishing firm here in Melbourne and we get special bulk purchase discounts for publishing. This way we can deliver the marketing and the leverage information in addition to getting the book done.

You can certainly walk into a publishing firm and get the package and get your book done, but one thing you may not get is the education around how to promote yourself. Book sales and the promotion of your intellectual property is totally up to you. I've read many articles and even traditional publishing houses don't really focus on pushing out and marketing your book. They might do it the first few weeks during the launch, but realistically you're responsible for that. That's why we pride ourselves on teaching that component.

I believe the value is more within that side of things than actually getting the book done, because hiring an editor or a proofreader is not really rocket science. How are you going to get to those million dollars in your coaching business and leverage through the other programs is where the absolute value and return on your investment lies.

Now that you have read this chapter, give yourself three tasks of what you're going to action. What kind of book will you write, will you unpack your book, will you set a schedule on how you're going to execute it? What are you going to write about? Who are you going to appeal to? It might not come to you straight away, just trust! I came up with the idea for this particular book, watching the movie *Rio 2* with my kids in the cinema 6 weeks ago. Just the title of it popped into my head when watching it and I wrote it down quickly in my notes on the iPhone and I'm trusting my gut that this is the right step that I'm taking. I did ask for feedback from people who said use weeks, months or years in the title, and for some reason

1000 days came to me and this is what I stand for. I know that 1000 days is around three years time and that is how long it's taken because it's one step and day at a time. That is exactly what you need to do.

	3 Actions I Commit to Taking to Create my Million Dollar Business	Done ✔
1		
2		
3		

Gift Resource to assist in your Development from reading this Chapter: 'Ultimate Book and Chapter Unpack Templates' as part of the Ultimate Million Dollar Coaching Business from Home Workbook available to download at: https://natasadenman.leadpages.net/milliondollarcoach/ or by scanning this QR Code with your phone.

Chapter 7

Leverage

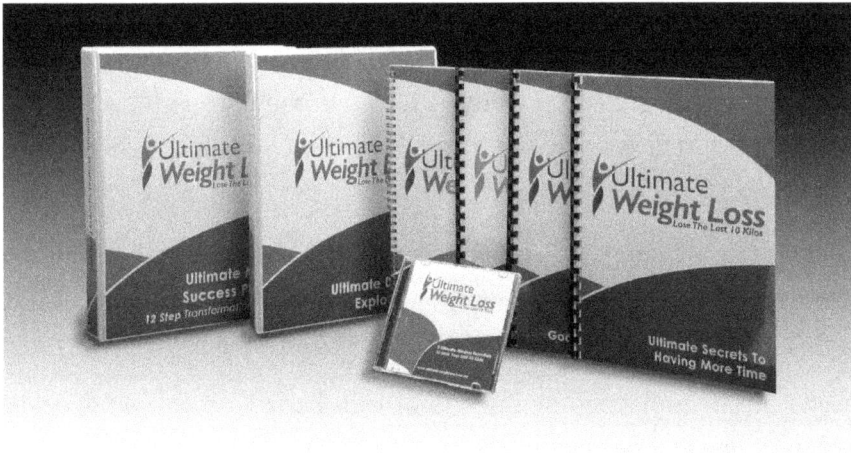

"Entrepreneurs must be willing to be misunderstood for LONG periods of time."
– Jeff Bezos

The authoring process was the first step to get recognition. To monetise and leverage that recognition is to pull together information from the book content and deliver it in the form of other products and programs. What I have learnt over the past 1000 days is that you can help people in so many other ways that a book can't possibly help them. A book generally will have a lot of information around why and what it is that people need to do, but it's impossible to put in all the detail of the how required to get people to their results. Unless you are planning to write a 500-page book that no one can be bothered reading. You may have noticed while reading this book, there are only a certain amount of words or explanations that I can give you within each of the sections. In reality I could write a whole book around each chapter alone. After all the *Ultimate 48 Hour Author* is a book purely focused on the authoring process which in this book is Chapter 6.

People will not get the help they need from you just by reading your book alone. That is just not going to cut it. I met one of my clients a while ago in Sydney and she said to me, 'You know what, Nat? Over the last couple of years I have followed you and bought all your books. Those books are fantastic, however had I done any of the work you suggested – no! I want you to hold my hand and show me how to do it for my individual circumstance.' I ended up working with her one on one for a while and assisted her in developing her how and intellectual property, which is now launched.

Remember, a book is just the starting point. I always talk about the sales funnel and that the book sits very high on your the sales funnel as a low entry point for people to start developing trust and intimacy with you.

What needs to happen by the end of your book is to give an awareness of what else you have on offer and through what programs and packages you can further help them. This should consist of those high-end programs, middle price range packages that people can opt in on. This will increase how many sales you make and will create different income streams within your business. It is only when you develop different income streams that you can leverage your business to 7 figures and beyond. One on one coaching alone will not be the answer alone. When you are just selling your time for money, you cannot make any more than a quarter of a million dollars unless your hourly rate is very high.

There are very successful coaches out there, who I have heard charge a million dollars per year for their coaching. Those people though have been around for decades in the industry, have a huge following and in reality don't promote one on one, which is exclusive to a few individuals that would invest at that level. If you are at a beginner level there is a different way of thinking and actions that are required to get to your first 7 figure year. To do that it is about how we implement and build infrastructure around different income streams in your business. Further product development beyond your book is the answer.

People vary in what we call their *convincer* strategies. Oftentimes they want to have more of a taste and an understanding of who you are. That's why having different levels of entry within your business is so important. For example, our signature program is the *Ultimate 48 Hour Author Retreat*, which is our highest end program. To close sales in this program it doesn't happen overnight. It sometimes takes months and maybe even years of nurturing a relationship with people who sometimes choose to do our inner circle or mastermind program. Others may have some mentoring or do another program until they are ready and at the point where they go yes, I trust you enough that you're going to take me on this journey and I'm going to be safe with you therefore I will invest and do the *Ultimate 48 Hour Author Retreat*.

That's what people want to know. Product development for coaches, consultants and mentors is very much around intellectual property and selling your thoughts. The types of products you can generate from your book and your core-content are E-books, audio books, workshops, webinars, retreats etc. Filming your workshops, retreats and webinars also allows for creation of video products that can be uploaded on hidden areas within You Tube and those links you can sell to people. I do on a consistent basis so I don't have to be in the room selling my time for money all of the time.

From the intellectual property that you have in your book you can structure the content of what you will assist people in doing if you were to work with them one on one, in groups, workshops, trainings or retreats, which is what we do.

Let's look a little bit further into what the sales funnel means and how to use the information from your book to bundle and package it up so that people have maximum value and really get value for this is way beyond your asking price.

Get a piece of paper and draw a funnel on it. At the widest part of your funnel you will have a lot of people who will take you up on free or low-cost offerings from your business. For example your book, a free report on your website are the kind of offers that sit at the top of your funnel. People are really testing the waters here and feel they are not threatened so they tend to say yes to the offer a lot more quickly.

As you go further down the funnel, you may have some low cost introductory programs like series of webinars, or a specific program that you sell, say at $97–$200. For these you actually still don't need to be in the room, people can purchase it off you online or via a connection on social media.

Further down might be your face to face workshops, training days and your lower cost events and after that the upsell to the high end programs.

At the bottom of the sales funnel is you. This is your one on one coaching and mentoring. The mistakes that I have seen a lot of coaches make from the early days is that they focus on selling their one on one first up. With one on one you need a lot of trust and a relationship to be present before someone says yes I'd love to have you as a one on one coach or mentor. If you are not getting results in getting those one on one clients, work out other ways you can build in more options within your sales funnel so that people have access to you in other ways and start to get to know you on a different level before taking the leap in working personally with you.

When they see the value, they won't object or hesitate in paying the price because they'll feel on some level they know you, trust you and like you and know the investment will be a worthwhile one.

With the information from your book, what I would suggest is taking each of the chapters and then implementing exercises. Design some templates, pull together information that people can actually take action on. The being comes with the doing. So get people to start taking action and doing things through tasks that you have pulled together. In your book you have been explained certain ways of getting things done. There are tools and strategies that you would have shared. The reality is those tools and strategies still have further steps to be broken down, so if you were to design a program manual from your book, what you do is go into each of those chapters and pull together information that people can actually work on when it comes to achieving the results you have thought.

Whether those will be exercises around their business or life, set some goals, create a vision board, whatever it is. For myself when I was speaking out the previous chapter, I was saying to you guys to unpack your intellectual property into 12 different steps. Put them in order, recreate new names so that your target market is being sold what they want and is being enticed and curious about the information that they're going to read, so that inside the content you can actually give them what they need.

This is how you expand from your book into other products and programs. This is why I recommend 12 chapter books, because 12 is a nice chunk for delivery of information. It's easily convertible to a 12-step program, a 12-

week program, a 12-month facilitation course, 12 webinars, 12 workshops, 12 E-books and the list goes on.

Don't be scared to rip off and duplicate your own intellectual property as it is all yours and you can do what you want with it. Be authentic with it and teach others what you have done, share your stories and truth and you will never have a problem. Blend your learnings from what you have studied, experienced and heard and tell it in your own voice. That is what makes it so unique and yours.

The best way is to let it come from the heart. Whatever it is that you need to say, you will say, you can on expand whatever feels right. When you get your transcripts back you can always change the words once you look at it in front of you, you can add different points and additional insights.

The last thing I wanted to discuss here is the bundling and packaging of your products and services. We are talking about product development in this chapter, which is the tangible nature of a coaching, mentoring or consulting business. The intangible nature is the delivery like your speaking events, one on one coaching, things that you do that people cannot touch and feel, but they get a lot of value from.

In bundling and packaging it is important to have a combination of both for maximum value. That way when people invest with you, you can give them a box of things like manuals, books and resources they can access in their own time. This way the value is perceived to be greater then purchasing the intangible service. When they get home and they're telling their family about the investment in your program and product and show what they get for it, it brings their family a lot more on board. They can physically see it and this makes it really powerful.

If you're a new coach there are also alternative ways to bring in tangible products in your packages. Simply use things that are not yours. For example, if a book has inspired you and changed your life in some way, why not buy five or ten of those books and have them as part of your packages. Use someone else's book before you have your own. I used to use another programs that I purchased to work with my clients up until the point when I had my own program.

In my weight loss niche I used to buy scales and heart rate monitor watches from eBay and then package them up because it had relevance within that particular niche. Coaches can give diaries to their clients. They can give gratitude journals or things like a planning template. You can walk into a stationery shop and buy some pretty awesome looking stationery. Especially if your clients are women they will appreciate it and can record the work they are doing with you on that stationery as it has that connection between you and them.

You can then walk into a $2 shop and buy a pretty box. They look nice, you can put all the products in it and when a client signs up for coaching with you, you can give them that as their starter pack. Really think about how you can create that wow experience. How can you give them more resources that they can use outside of working with you? When you have developed the other programs and products you will start giving them those. When our *Ultimate 48 Hour Authors* come to the weekend, they get the *Ultimate Product Generator* manual, the *Ultimate 48 Hour Author* book and the *Ninja Couch Marketing book*, which are all relevant to what they're about to learn. At the end of the experience they get their book and access to all the people that we have hired on their behalf to save them a lot of time and money on sourcing all that on their own.

As bonuses, everything that I have recorded ever and my inner circle membership comes as a lifetime membership for all of our authors. They get hours upon hours of trainings, workshops and content that I have delivered, that they can choose to immerse themselves to learn, execute and build that million dollar coaching business for themselves.

The value in all these resources is in the 6 figures versus the actual investment that they're making in the program. I always say as we grow, we are going to bring these resources to you as additional value through your journey. So not just the first 6–12 months of us dealing with you but for life. How awesome is that!

Some of the things that people have a real aversion to when it comes to product development is that they're scared that if they invest all this time in creating high end programs, what happens if no-one buys it? What I say to that is no intellectual property is ever wasted. What we can do is change it up, rename it, create something new. After all, I've said it before and will say it again, nothing is new in this world, everything is repackaged and put in a different way. Then give it a sexy name. Add more to your intellectual property, change your copy in your sales letter for that particular program and see how it goes by re-launching it.

If it's not working, ask for feedback from the people who are saying no to your programs and work out how you can recreate them and present them again. You don't need to start from scratch every single time. You can leverage your intellectual property in other ways just by changing the make-up of it.

Other people say that they just don't have the time to build product. They are busy parents and are still working in a day job. Product development is the last thing they think about. What I would then do is focus on scheduling those events and webinars and create your offers just on paper before you go about creating them. Sell them first then create them. When I created the *Ultimate 48 Hour Author weekend*, I did not have anything ready bar my table of value, which would show what people would get as their tangibles and intangibles and the outcome. Once I sold the first package and subsequently the first 10, which created the first group of authors for that particular retreat, I started focusing on pulling together the manual and the PowerPoint, all the systems around it. When people invest in you and make the commitment to you, you will be compelled to stick out your commitment and promise to them. When you sell your programs and packages and they're just on paper as an offer, you won't procrastinate over creating them, because of the commitment that somebody has made to you and you have made to them.

If you're feeling stuck in what would work best for you, work out what your values are, speak to a mentor or take action adjusting along the way to find out what's the best fit. You know my story, which started out as generalist life coach and working out that health and wellness was the first niche I wanted to help people in. Fine tuning that to lose the last 10 kilos, then getting into product development and author mentoring –what a diverse journey it has been.

You are an entrepreneur. Your journey today is not going to be the same in the next 12–18 months. That's okay because you will evolve and grow and you will bring more value through that constant and never ending improvement that you will be going through. Embrace that and everything you can create along the way will be able to be used in some way. My husband recreated our weight-loss mindset manual by changing the examples and stories in it, so that it was relevant to business owners. We had one program for our Business-coaching niche in a box and by doing this we ended up with 2 programs in just 24 hours because of that recreation.

Products are fun to make. Make it your goal to make three new products every year and before you know it, you will have an abundance of products and programs that you can actually pick and choose from. Then you can create your bundles without having to create anything for a while. Trust me, it does get addictive. You will want to create new things over time. As you grow you will want to teach that to people.

Right now, write down the three things that you will action as a result of reading this chapter in the spaces below and go forth leveraging your business to the next level.

3 Actions I Commit to Taking to Create my Million Dollar Business		
		Done ✔
1		
2		
3		

Gift Resource to assist in your Development from reading this Chapter: Sample Coaching Packages and Tables of Value to Model as part of the Ultimate Million Dollar Coaching Business from Home Workbook available to download at: https://natasadenman.leadpages.net/milliondollarcoach/ or by scanning this QR Code with your phone.

Chapter 8
Money

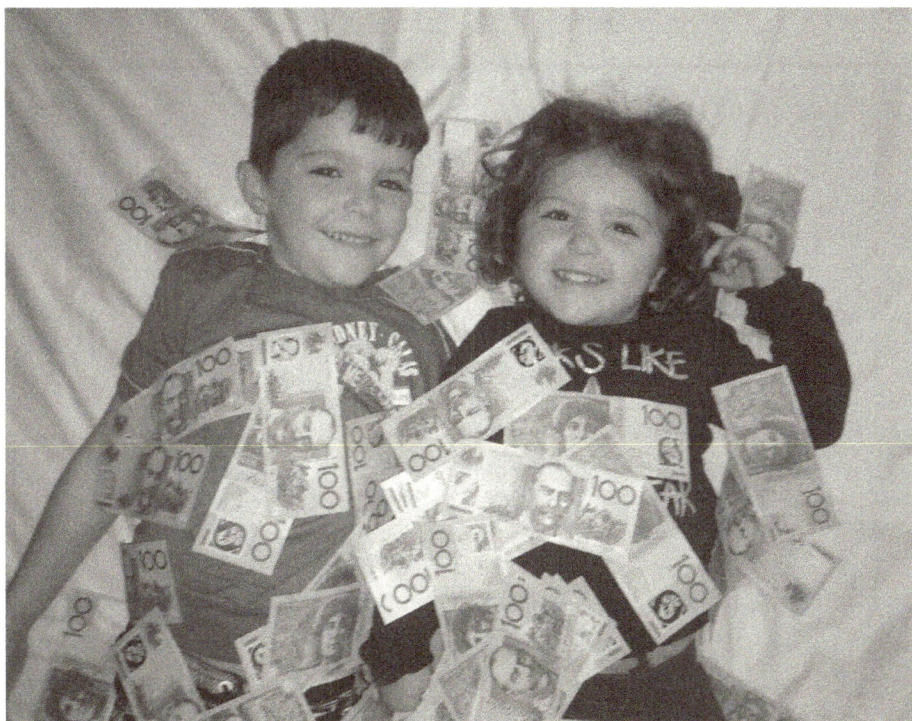

"Be in control of your money. If you are not in full control of your money while dealing with it – be it in earning, saving, protecting, budgeting, investing, insuring, etc. – then it will control you and you will never be able to achieve financial independence."

– Bill Gates

Ignorance is bliss, knowledge is power.

Many business owners that I have met along my journey have been oblivious to what kind of revenue they're generating. They don't pay attention to their numbers within their business because of the sheer fact that there's nothing coming in. I can say that was myself early on in this journey before my mentor said to me that I should start a weekly dashboard to track my numbers.

He said to me to get into the habit of putting together what I was spending and what I was earning. For months the earning part of my spreadsheet had nothing on it, yet the expenses were a lot. I did keep a basic Excel spreadsheet in a display book where I could flip through the weeks and see how I was progressing in the business. It was a manual system. Nowadays with all the accounting software that we have available to us, we can see so many different reports that give us awareness of our numbers. We can see the GST, the expenses and the sales and income for each week, month or year. We can identify what income streams and type of expenses we have along the way and work out what our bottom line is. In the early days I didn't have anything like that. I purely kept a spreadsheet on my computer, which was still a great start.

The other thing that my mentor said to me was to start a marketing dashboard as well to see what marketing activities we were putting out there and how they are measuring up in terms of response rates and effectiveness.

These two habits were really fantastic to get good at when there wasn't huge numbers to deal with like there are today. In business there's a saying and every accounting and finance person will tell you that 'Cash flow is King.' It is so important to know when your business becomes viable and for yourself to understand where to budget, how much to budget and how to put aside some money for investments in the future.

Business is an investment. We build it so that one day the sale of it has made it all worthwhile. Down the track when you are ready to exit your business you'll want to walk away with a little nest egg for yourself because of what you've been building over the years.

If you want success in business and you want to help many others, money must become part of your top three values. If we don't think about money and we don't look at where our situation is, then it's unlikely that it's going to be within our focus that we achieve the targets that we set for ourselves. You need to start to have an understanding of your spending power versus what you need to survive.

This is what I call your 'core expenses.' If you are serious about understanding your numbers, you are guaranteed that you end up with the mature approach of a serious business owner instead of one that sees their business as just a hobby as much as they'd like to think that it is not.

If you don't focus on knowing your numbers, failure is imminent, bankruptcy probable. Stress, anxiety and depression are at high alert. If you don't love money, why would money love you back? Just think about it like this – if you don't love your partner, why would they stick around and stay with you? And neither will money. A lot of us have been raised with a lot of limiting beliefs around money. The common sayings of, 'money doesn't grow on trees', 'rich people are bad people', 'money is the root of all evil'. There was even a saying in Macedonia that literally translated meant 'money is a killer'.

If you had all of this embedded into your subconscious mind from a very young age, you would have set up a certain money blueprint that you keep bringing into reality. This means there's no way to break through that unless you start changing your underlying beliefs around money. There are many people that think that those people who become millionaires do so overnight. That is not true. I believe over a period of time as you start earning more, you start finding new levels of lifting that money barometer higher and higher for yourself.

What used to be $50,000 per year in wages was a lot of money for me at one stage, no longer seems to be even a scratch on the surface within a month nowadays. Every single year as I grow and expand my barometer gets slightly higher and I become more comfortable in generating those new levels of income and being able to value myself. Because of this I also price myself according to my growth. As you grow in confidence and self-worth, you bring more value to the table and you will build more value into your business. That is why you should charge more the longer you have been in your coaching business.

Work out what you need to keep afloat in your business and in your life. Do this for your life first. What I'd like to give you here is a very basic budget template that I have used over the years, that really shows you whether you're living above or below your means. You can see straight away if you are overspending or underspending. Most of the time people find out that they are overspending and they need to cut back on certain areas that they didn't know they were spending so much on. In the resources pack that I've got prepared for you, you will find this budget template. It's a basic spreadsheet where you can document everything that's coming in and going out and figure out if there are areas you can cut down on and then invest that in other business building activities that are going to generate greater cash flow at the other end.

You need to also start measuring your actions with money that is going in and out of your business on a weekly basis. That's why in the resources pack I'll put in the initial spreadsheet that I used to do my weekly expenses and income and also the marketing dashboard. This is a very basic concept of what I was putting out there and also gave me personal accountability where I would see what marketing I was doing and the results from it. I could see if I was putting out enough content, going networking and seeking different opportunities to tell people about my business.

The last thing you need to do in understanding your numbers is to start getting comfortable with making some sacrifices early on, so that you can build that ideal lifestyle you desire a lot quicker. I remember in my first 12 months, it was very difficult to spend any money, certainly not on myself, but even on my son. I remember my mum buying him clothes and one day I was really getting upset and whining to my husband that I couldn't even buy him a toy. At the same time, I was obviously investing in my education, programs and in my mentor, which is where the bulk of my money went. Looking in hindsight, I'm very proud of myself to have sacrificed those few months or even the first year to achieve the knowledge that I did to build my business.

Nowadays when we walk into shops, we barely even look at price points. We just pick up what we want, the kids get whatever it is they need to a certain extent as we don't want to teach them that they can get everything every single time. Certainly we believe in rewards, we believe in getting what we need when we need it and celebrating the successes along the way.

Knowing your numbers is one of the key components for your success. It appears late in this book, but it's something that should be happening right from the word 'go'. You might be further along in your business and you are already measuring your numbers. The decision is whether you outsource your bookkeeping or you do it yourself. Personally I do my own bookkeeping because at the end of each month I sit down with my husband and we do all our reconciliations from our previous month. The beauty of doing that ourselves is that we keep a tight system around who needs to get their receipts and what expenses have gone through the business. It makes us keep our finger on the pulse for the best of our business and financial health.

If you do it regularly, it doesn't have to take very long. I often think, why do people hire bookkeepers when it takes me at the most a couple of hours at the end of the month to put in all the ins and outs of the business and we have a lot of fun looking at our reports afterwards. We look at what we have we done month-to-date, year-to-date and how that compared to last year. We look at what our tax bill is going to potentially look like, what we have to pay to the government so that we know that a certain amount of our cash flow will be diminished by things like a GST and tax bill.

It's rewarding but it's not for everyone. If you absolutely hate bookkeeping and accounting, then make the decision to outsource it because you will not do it justice. However, if you're a person who likes numbers and want to see how you're progressing and want a real time view of what is going on then I would advise you to do your own bookkeeping. Schedule the third or fourth day into the next month as a day where you will spend a couple of hours on your numbers and accounting.

If you have a business that generates a lot of sales, perhaps lower cost sales and higher volume, then bookkeeping can become tedious than in a business where you are dealing with higher dollar sales and lower volume that makes it's a lot easier to manage on the bookkeeping front. There are different things that suit different businesses and varied amounts of time that it will take to generate the reports and the bookkeeping. You can hire a bookkeeper that does it regularly for you every month and they send you reports and to look at those for you to get to know your numbers.

Each to their own, use your skills and your strengths where you love what you're doing. In my case, sitting down to do bookkeeping and accounting has been an enjoyable task in the business. If it's not enjoyable then don't do it. Certainly, if you cannot outsource it due to cost restrictions and the like you have to learn to do it. It's really good to know how to do it yourself so you have a basic understanding of what's going on with your business.

Some of the questions that might pop up in your mind or you're experiencing could be – what if I haven't got enough to cover my core? What if I am living above my means? I do meet business owners who are fulltime in their businesses, and they keep trying to make their business a success while living off their partner's income. In this situation, I say maybe you should consider getting a part-time job that's not in the key hours you would build your business. For example, I used to work part-time on a Sunday, Monday and Thursday. Sunday and Monday weren't a busy day for building a business but they were providing enough cash flow to cover my mentoring and education expenses and then the core or our living expenses was covered by my husband's wage.

You can always cut down somewhere within your budget. A part-time job should not be something that you're disappointed in having to get through the survival stage of your business. It's actually an admirable decision to keep you afloat until the business gets to a level where you can completely let go. I let go of my part-time job when I was generating double the amount of income that I was earning in that part-time job. My husband let go of his full-time job when we were generating three times the income he was making in his current management job. That had to be consistent at least over a three-month period for us to be confident enough that we could survive just solely on the business.

There was definitely a transition period. There wasn't a leap of faith by quitting in the beginning, which is what sometimes people do. I personally am not the biggest risk-taker. I would say I'm a moderate risk-taker and have always made sure that there's some kind of a buffer when I am going out to do something that potentially might affect my family.

If your partner is not on board for your journey in your business and doesn't believe in investing in mentors or programs for you to develop, then what

I suggest is start educating them on what you're doing. Get them involved and talk about your progress in the work that you're implementing. When they agree on an investment for you to get a mentor or invest in a program, make them proud by showing them the actions that you're taking. When people will invest and then they don't take action, their partner feels like the money's gone down the drain and they're less likely to support them the next time around. What you will find is that when they know what you are and actions are taken, they can see progress and they will be willing to say yes again for future business investments.

If you have poor beliefs about money and always end up in the same position, which is very often broke, I would invest some reading time on where this comes from. What is your money blueprint and really start to stretch out that range where you allow abundance to come to you. You need to respect money, because when it is being respected, I believe the universe gives you more. By managing it, if you cannot manage money, you're not going to get given more. The more money you make, the higher the expenses. It's not like you have a million dollar business and you still have only $30 000 a year in expenses. The higher your income, the higher your outgoings are as well, which means what we used to get as income in the early days in the hundreds of dollars and expenses were also in the hundreds. When we get income in the thousands there's usually expenses in the thousands as well.

It's all relative and certainly the profit margin is a lot bigger, however you will never be able to build a hugely successful business that brings in a lot of cash flow, unless you show that you can manage that very cash flow. Otherwise if you get into trouble, bankruptcy could be on the horizon very quickly which will ruin your business and affect your life.

My parting words for this chapter are to understand your core needs. Work out where you can sacrifice some of the income so that you can build your business a lot faster. Invest in the right areas. We always have to

Chapter 9

Exposure

"Speech is power: speech is to persuade, to covert, to compel."
– Ralph Waldo Emerson

One of the crucial components in becoming and leveraging a business to 7-figures is people knowing you, seeing you, spending time with you and really getting to know the value that you bring. With exposure through becoming a speaker online and offline, you will build positioning and further your expertise around what you talk about. I'm a big believer that externalizing your expertise is so important in gaining new insights and being able to become an amazing communicator.

This is one of the reasons I also speak out my books and I'm consistently looking for opportunities to speak. By doing that, I start to become a person who can be understood by more than 95% of people. I have seen people speak and the audience's eyes glaze over because the information they deliver is not relevant or understood by everyone in the room. To become a master communicator you have to do what master communicators do, which is continuously speak about what you're passionate about. With doing that you'll build your confidence and certainty around your content, as well as coming up with insights. When we gain exposure and are running many events the best bonus about it is we expand our intellectual property and we learn from others and ourselves each and every time. Then we build on what we already have and always keep it fresh which also builds stamina and the ability to deliver content. I remember when I started out I used to worry about delivering a 30–45 minute segment. Slowly I started delivering 90 minutes and then expanded that to a half-day event and then eventually full-day events and weekend retreats. I now have so much content and so many skills, steps and formulas in my mind that I could speak for a week. With my clients I could be training them, developing their mindset, building their businesses, working on their credibility, their products and delivering marketing education.

Exposure is so important. It is not just about gaining more business, leads, prospects and clients, but more for your own growth and expansion of your intellectual property. I often hear people say with every training that we run, if you attend the training this week or next week you'll get different insights. When we read a book we've read before, we're looking at it from a different perspective because we are at a different stage in our life. It's never understood exactly the same and we pick up different meanings from it. That's the same as being a person that delivers the content in your speaking events. You will always bring up a different story or metaphor and a different angle to what you're saying every time you present. This also has got to do with the participation of the people in the audience. That's the beauty of what makes it so unique and so special when you run events and become a speaker.

To gain exposure for yourself and your business there are a few different ways that you can do it. Some ways are easier to execute and others more challenging. In this chapter I want to focus on the four different areas I have gained exposure around my brand and business and how you can do it for yourself. Those four areas are:

- Workshops

- Networking events

- Webinars

- Speaking engagements

Speaking gigs are generally the most challenging to get your foot in the door with however, once you do, that particular events organizer manages the invites of the attendees as well as the promotion of you before the event. Let's start from the first one on the list and explain how I have been able to do that and how you can replicate it for yourself and your business.

Workshops

Workshops were the very first thing that I started doing in my business. One of my biggest things I see with workshops is a lot of people have the intention of doing them but they keep procrastinating. My very first tip for you is when it comes to events, you must just set the date before anything else! Whether it is a booking for a speaking event it doesn't matter even if it's 4-6 months down the track it comes around very fast. Always set the date first. With workshops I would set the date and book a venue around 6 weeks ahead of time. If they are bigger events like retreats or anything longer than a day, I would give it more time, about 2–3 months ahead of time is the rule. All our *Ultimate 48 Hour Author retreats* are pre-scheduled for the next 12 months so people know the dates and they can plan and lock out their spots ahead of time.

The very next thing that needs to happen is to come up with sexy names and copy around what you will deliver. We have talked about the concept of 'sell them what they want, give them what they need' so using hypnotic words and phrases, tap into that emotional centre of what people want from you. When you do this you will get a lot more people coming to your workshop then just calling your workshop 'Goal-Setting' instead of 'Design Your Ideal Future.'

The most time you will spend when it comes to organizing a workshop is around getting bums on seats. When you are organizing to fill your workshop 90% of your effort will be to fill the room. The other 10% will be creating a flyer, booking the venue, coming up with the content and delivering the workshop. The focus needs to lie in getting people into the room. My suggestion around this is to offer bonuses and specials to entice people to sign up. Think about what you could offer such as a buy one get one free ticket or an early bird special. I usually give away a bonus of my book when people come to my events. Whichever one is most relevant to that particular audience and what the event is about.

Then you really need to think about what your upsell is. An upsell is the call to action at the end of your workshop. If you are early on in business I want to give you a big tip here. If people come into a free or low-cost event don't upsell them to a $5,000–$10,000 program. You most likely don't have the sales skills and the language around getting people so excited that they pull out their credit card and invest in those high-end programs. What worked for me early on, and I even use it today, as I love to build the relationship a lot more before offering that high-end program, is to offer what that very next step after the free or low cost workshop is. Could your upsell be a little package bundle, something you can offer that's low-cost, low-risk or you end up spending some one-on-one time with the person that wants to take the next step to really help them in an individual way. Then you can figure out where they would fit into your sales funnel understanding what the next step for them could be. Sometimes the attendees may not be suitable for your program. They might need to go into some form of membership for a little while, or get some other experience before they are ready for your programs. That strategy is what I have found to convert the most from my teaser workshops.

Webinars

When you have a bigger network and access to a large group of people, start running webinars. Webinars are a lot quicker to organise. You are in and out within 7–10 days. You do all the promotion, run the call and follow through with what you have promised, and have an upsell. I suggest making them free. Once again you need to come up with a sexy name and copy that is hypnotic enough to get people to say, 'I want to be on that call or I want to find out what this particular system or formula is.' The best way I have found to fill my webinars has been blasting it out through social media, sending it out to my e-mail list and also running some paid advertising via social media or Google Adwords. Social media is great to get people signed up and registered. One thing to know with webinars is that if you see 100 people registered; don't think that 100 people are going to turn up live.

Expect about 50% show up rate. The rest of the people will go onto your list and you can communicate to them and you can send out a recording after the webinar. Those who are live on the call will also be the most likely ones to take that next step with you. Make the upsell relevant, again low-cost and low-risk so that you can secure a conversation with those people that are interested. With webinars, because people are not in the room with you, they have less attachment and less trust and intimacy with you. You have really got to be great at executing your upsell in the offer to that next step by delivering tones of value without giving away too much 'how' as the 'how' is the next step and your upsell. Running webinars also builds further trust in the community around those who are following you.

Networking

When your network grows bigger you can consider running your own networking events. Around 18 months ago, I launched a Facebook group, called Ultimate Business Support. (You are welcome to join us there and interact with us) I had built up enough of a following of people I had met out and about that I decided to start my own networking event in addition to the Facebook group. This Facebook group, at the time of writing this book has around 6,500 members. To compliment that, we run an offline event, also called Ultimate Business Support, in Melbourne. Once you have been out and about regularly and you have built a lot of relationships and a good network, then a networking event with your flavour is a great way for positioning yourself in a leadership role. You then get to speak, practice your speaking and presenting on your terms as no-one can tell you what you can do at your own networking event. I suggest that you always have some kind of role when you speak to your audience and you keep building that muscle. It makes you a connector of people. You connect others and then you're also being connected yourself to other people because of the opportunity that you have created with your event. I can guarantee you will generate lots of business due to the positioning and you get to make the rules.

Think about your format, your structure and why people would want to come to your event. What is the value that you're bringing? You could even treat it as similar to a workshop. If you run it like we have which is more into an educational focus, then it's more like a workshop. My recommendation is to run the event monthly.

It takes a lot of responsibility and focus because these will come around quickly and filling them can be a challenge. A couple of tips where we expand and grow our numbers are that in the beginning of the week that the event is running, we will give three free tickets away to people who have never attended it. By doing this it gets them to experience the event for the first time and it builds our list. When you're running a networking event, you want to build a database of people who attend it and then that database of people you send out a regular e-mail reminder when your next event is approaching. What used to be a lot of work with chasing people up to fill our event in the first 5–6 months, in the last 12 months has been quite easy. You might like to have a membership structure for your event. We have chosen to do it very casually, no strings attached or commitment and a wonderful variety of people are coming along. Be patient with your events. Build your list and you might even offer some half-priced tickets if you want to drive numbers further. You can also do a buy one ticket, bring a friend for free.

Speaking Engagements

One of the awesome things that I have seen people with and I've encouraged my clients to do is to have a speaker bio. The best speaker bio is an A4 size with three of your key topics you speak on written out in a hypnotic way that is attractive for any potential event organiser. Make sure you get it professionally designed unless you are a wiz with formatting. Get your compelling bio on the left hand side of the page. Then add your picture, your contact details and any credibility building badges, like newspapers, TV or radio you have appeared in. If you have written a book you could add that as well to boost your credibility as someone who will be highly considered as a speaker. Eventually I would invest in a speaker bio video, which is like a trailer of you speaking in front of an audience. This is something that comes with time and I wouldn't do it straight away. An A4 flyer that describes you as a speaker would be something that you can create easily and for just $5 via Fiverr.com. Put your hand up and be prepared to speak for free in the beginning. Even if it's free this is invaluable exposure.

I have travelled interstate so many times and paid for my own travel and accommodation just to get put in front of people. It's really awesome when you're going interstate, as it's has special kind of connection. People say wow, she's come to speak to us and it makes it a little more unique and a lot of business has come from those opportunities. Be prompt in submitting all your information when people ask you to speak and ask lots of questions around what you can and can't do. This is very important, especially around the call to action. Are you allowed to have a call to action? Can you give people any gifts? Can you donate a door prize? Take the initiative to make the organiser's life easy. After the event, make sure you follow-up within 24–48 hours and send out any gifts you've promised. Add people to your database and continue building those relationships, as they may not result in sales immediately. I can guarantee you if you keep in touch with them, they will come back in due course when they're ready to work with you. That's what relationship marketing is about after all.

One tip I want to share with you is how to capture details from people in the room when you don't have the opportunity to get the whole list from the organiser. Most times you can give them something for free. You could say, 'Who here wants some free stuff?' As I've got all my books available in e-book format, I'd say who would like a copy from my *Ultimate 48 Hour Author E-book*. Most people would put their hand up. I then get them to text their name and e-mail address to my mobile number and by the next day they will have it in their inbox and they will be able to read it on their iPad or Kindle. Most people, in fact 80% of people will do that as everyone wants to get valuable resources especially if the person in front of them is positioned as an expert and they've grown to like and trust them during the talk.

Things that come up for business owners early and even as they're building their businesses is that fear of *what if no one comes?* This is a valid fear. I have it come up for me time and time again even though I know there's a lot of people who turn up to my events because of the positioning and expertise and exposure that I've built for myself. One beautiful thing that I heard from a client of mine was that when the first person registers I celebrate and it doesn't matter if it's just that one person, because wow, what value they will get. I think the same way, but the way she put it was like celebrate even when that one person signs up for your event. If you need to get some more people in the room, have you got some friends, who could come? Just know that they will get tons of value from you. Once I did a workshop in front of one person at a chiropractic centre and my mum happened to come that day. The chiropractor and the assistant sat down and all of a sudden I had 4 and that one actual attendee took up my $7,000 annual coaching program that I had at the time. That was actually the biggest win I had with the smallest amount of people in an audience.

If you don't know where to look for speaking events, just ask around. Go networking and ask at networking events. A lot of people will show you or tell you of certain places and you just need to keep asking. Many networking events have speakers and that is the first place that I would start out to look. They are generally not scary and they're a more supportive environment then official groups/associations and are always looking for high-value content. I am consistently having people come up to me, saying they would like to speak at my event. When you are approaching event organisers, always look at what value you will bring, how you will serve and will it fit the structure and what they stand for.

The last thing is that some people are terrified of speaking and it's commonly said to be the second worst fear other than death. All I can say to that is every talk that you do, the next one will be easier, and the next one even easier. You will be more fluent, use less notes and aids helping you get through your talks. You will soon just be able to get up and speak on your feet as when you keep externalizing the information, similar content and questions will arise for people, you can just pick them up on the spot and answer them. The more you practice, the less preparation time is required so much even down to none in some instances. You will just rock up and do what you need to do and then keep going. I always suggest to capture people's details that attend your talk and to have a call to action and to focus on serving those in the room, because they will come and ask what they can do further with you.

Now, write down the three things you will do as a result of reading this chapter. I've delivered a lot and there are a lot of areas where you can expand and research a lot more yourself so that you have a more detailed way of executing them. If you do all four of these things, workshops, webinars, networking and speaking engagements, your business will grow exponentially. You want to be setting up all your calendar and campaigns around these things six months in advance and be booking these events in, as these are your opportunities to generate more sales and continue building that network of people following you and knowing about you.

3 Actions I Commit to Taking to Create my Million Dollar Business		
		Done ✔
1		
2		
3		

Gift Resource to assist in your Development from reading this Chapter: 'Ultimate Book and Chapter Unpack Templates' as part of the Ultimate Million Dollar Coaching Business from Home Workbook available to download at: https://natasadenman.leadpages.net/milliondollarcoach/ or by scanning this QR Code with your phone.

Chapter 10
Online

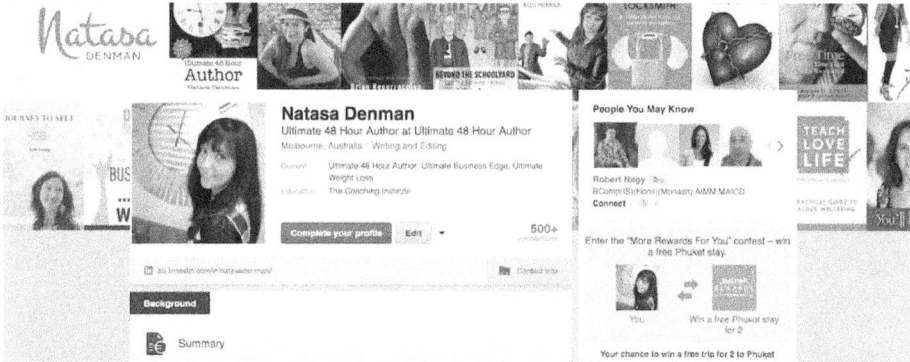

*"If your business is not on the internet, then your business will
be out of business."*
– Bill Gates

We have spoken a lot about offline relationships and the beauty of today's world is that we now have the opportunity to take those offline relationships and continue nurturing them online. Online nurturing of relationships usually occurs via the various social media platforms. For those of you who are a bit averse to technology and social media I want you to consider the benefit of learning how to become online savvy.

Online you can reach a wider audience for your business than just your local 18–50 km radius that you can access offline. You can keep in touch with people a lot more regularly than the limitations that we have with face-to-face interactions. Ultimately it's about building that global business, that can operate anywhere in the world, especially if you are a coach, consultant or a mentor – the world is your oyster.

Last year alone, I went away with my mum and spent some time in Greece, Italy and Macedonia. I was away for 5 weeks from home. I only had about 7–10 days of non-business time while we were travelling through Italy. The rest of the time I would do some of the work through the hotels we stayed in Greece and Macedonia. It was wonderful and super flexible. To make that a reality was one of my first visions for my business. I set that as one of my earliest intentions to build a coaching business that I can run from anywhere in the world especially my aunties kitchen table in Macedonia. I have done that multiple times now.

The online world is also amazing for building a community that gets tons of value from you. That way when you get a bigger following, you can organise to meet up face to face. One of the things that is wonderful about social media is that you get access to people you wouldn't normally meet.

Connections with influential people who you otherwise wouldn't get to meet in real life become a real possibility to connect with online and start a conversation. An example that I have had is with one of my biggest mentors in my life that prompted and planted a seed around what I have done today – Terry Hawkins. Terry Hawkins has a business called People in Progress and she moved from Australia over to the US to build her business further. I ended up finding her on Facebook and told her the difference that she had made with me 8–9 years ago when she had spoken at one of my work conferences. The conversation unfolded that way and before I knew it she was coming down for a 3-day training in Melbourne. This was a rarity, as I had never seen her doing anything like that. I put my hand up to on the crew (help out) at her event via a private message in hope to get to be in the room with her, because at the time I didn't have the cash flow to pay to attend this particular training.

I think it was around the $3,000. She didn't respond for a little while and with a couple of days from that particular training she got back to me in haste. She apologised that she had missed my message and that she would love to have me crew at the event to help out with logistics. I got to spend 3 intense days with her in the room with just 20 people. This was very special as the first time I saw her presenting it was in front of a thousand people. I got to know her more over the 3 days and vice versa and we've kept that relationship going for the past 3 years.

Those are just some of the little bonuses and perks of reaching out and offering help to people – even those you admire and perhaps you feel intimidated by. Not everyone is going to have the outcome that I have had in most cases. The power of online connection and nurturing that relationship opened up the door to that opportunity. If you don't focus at least on some level online with your business and the community that you're building, you will miss out on a huge share of the ideal customers from all over the world. You will limit your business growth to the local area and your relationship building will be slower and more confined locally. There are three different ways I would like to discuss with you around building and utilising your online strategies. They are: social media, website and your customer relationship management system.

Social Media

As a coach, consultant or a mentor I recommend the most valuable networks to be active on are Facebook, LinkedIn and YouTube.

With YouTube you can post videos on your channel and share them on your other social media platforms. Nowadays there is an option on most platforms to upload your videos directly, which works a lot better in terms of your post being shown to as many people as possible. There are so many social media platforms and people get confused which one to use. The ones that I will talk about are the ones I've been successful in leveraging. Also it is best to do a few well than 10 haphazardly.

Let's look at Facebook first. Facebook is a really good platform for your local and national connections due to time zone limitations. LinkedIn is the same but I've also found that LinkedIn is really good for starting the international connections and conversations. The results that I've been able to generate from being part of the LinkedIn forums have been an amazing amount of conversations with people internationally. With Facebook, I feel like it's my lounge room where I can go and hang out with people that I've known personally in my life but I've also expanded my network there beyond just the personal connections and strategically connected with people who I've met out and about. And I usually do that after an event within 24–48 hours of meeting someone.

That way they still remember me and accept me as a connection/friend. I then nurture that relationship through inviting people to be part of my Facebook community group called Ultimate Business Support, which is at 6,500 members at the time of writing of this book.

The steps I take are to first make the connection, then the nurturing of that relationship comes from adding value through posts that are relevant to my community. It's not just posts about me or what I have to sell, but humanising my posts and sharing a little bit about my life, what I do, about my children and certainly adding aspects of what my goals are and what I am looking to achieve. I share tips and insights from what is happening around our businesses that people can get value from instantly.

It's also really great to mix up your posts between written posts, picture posts and video posts and be mindful in sharing a lot of external links, because sometimes links are not favoured by social media platforms, which means not many people will see them.

Be mindful that social media platforms do change the rules very regularly in terms of what they will allow people to do versus what they won't allow them to do. Also what they prefer to show. For example in the past your business fan page was seen by a lot of people that liked it, but nowadays, Facebook prefers to show only paid, boosted ads to people of the relevant audience selected in the ad. It's become a platform where they're prioritising people who are paying for advertising to get exposure. Often people ask me about the importance of having a fan page and I believe that they are still important to have even if your posts don't get shown to many people. They are not the be-all and end-all of your business success. You must have one because it's like your website on social media. In addition to having a business fan page, I would recommend that you visit the interactive 2-way conversation pages, like groups or forums where you will get the most results. This is where you truly get conversations going.

A rule of thumb that I always have for social media is the minute someone connects with me, I will always send them an inbox message, which is a private message, to say hello. I ask what was it about my profile that prompted them to connect. This is what I use on LinkedIn or on Facebook; 'Have we met somewhere? I can see we have a few mutual connections; just wondering, how we've come across one another.' Generally this will start a conversation, which means I am not just clicking accept and increasing my numbers on these platforms but trying to make a real connection.

There's so much that has been written on social media by experts. In summary make sure that your profiles are set up correctly, especially on LinkedIn. It's very powerful to have a strong profile where people have endorsed you for a lot of things. Ask people to write recommendations for you on your profile because those recommendations you can cut and paste anywhere else for further promotion and building of your profile. Your profile must be connected to your websites and actually on your website so that people can look you up. All visuals like your cover photo, your personal profile picture, which looks professional and clear are really important to put out a positive and professional image. Please don't put up a picture of your cat on the profile. As a coach, consultant, or mentor, I strongly recommend that you represent the person that your ideal client wants to become.

Another important aspect of social media is that you respond to people quickly and that you look at helping people and practice patience. In the early days, it will seem like no one notices what you are doing, no one is commenting on your stuff, but as you consistently turn up over a period of time, you will notice that the interactions will increase and the enquiries will start coming in more frequently.

Every week I get someone enquiring about a product, service or program that we've got offering through a private message on LinkedIn or Facebook. In the past it used to happen once every six months or so. The time frame will shorten the more patient you are. The key to it is to be consistent and to be there present adding value at least five out of seven days a week.

Now for one little disclaimer here is that social media can become very distracting to an individual so you've got to be mindful to plan your time wisely. You must plan your social media strategy for your business as it can eat away so much productive business time when you're constantly taken away from your focused activities, looking at notifications, what messages are coming through. Did you know that it takes you 15 minutes to get back on focus with a task when you have been distracted by something? Keep that in mind, because how many times could you possibly get distracted in a day? It can easily add up to 2–3 hours of wasted time.

I normally deal with my social media for half an hour in the morning and half an hour in the evening. Most people will be on at those particular times for my target market. If your target market has different patterns, research this and choose to be on there when they are.

Turn off your notifications for your emails and your Facebook and LinkedIn. Only go in there, checking them when you're ready to check them, rather than having little beeps and buzzes that come up on your phone consistently taking you away from what you're working on, which I am trusting is going to be a money-making exercise.

Website

The other way to connect with people online is through your website. I assume you are a coach, consultant or a mentor – you're not a website developer. It's great to have techie skills to some level, but mastering the art of search engine optimisation or keywords, running ads, paid ads online or website design – that's not your strength.

Outsource those things to other people to take care of for you and if you're early on in your business and you don't have the resources to be able to do that, then you can hire people via Elance.com at a very low cost to begin with. This is what I did before hiring people locally to have the basics set up.

A very basic but great looking website that you can do yourself for free using your Linkedin Profile can be created via Strikingly.com. You can choose to purchase $96 package for the whole year of them hosting a proper domain name. For myself I set up NatasaDenman.com and with that $96 you get your one domain name included with all the hosting. You plug in your LinkedIn profile and you can then fine-tune it yourself really easily before you make it go live. It can't get any cheaper than that and the websites look really slick and professional. It's literally a 1-click website and it gets created so quickly. It has a contact form at the bottom and people scroll through the different sections. It just all appears on one long page. The totally free version would just have Strikingly within the domain name plus your name in the URL.

If you are going to hire someone to help you with your website, one of the key components you want to have is a call to action. When people arrive at your website, you want to have something that they can give you their details for, so that they receive a free report or template, a tool, a test, whatever it is that you can create that is of value, that's going to solve your target market's problem. What we're looking for is a resource that's going to give them **results in advance**. For example, How to lose 5 kilos in 3 days or 3 secrets to losing 5 kilos in 3 days.

It's measurable, it tells them what they're going to achieve at the end of reading the resource guide. When creating one ask yourself – Does my resource give my ideal client some results in advance so they're interested in finding out more beyond that? What this process does, is make people give you their contact details for your database. This way you can continue communicating with them through your database, it keeps them within your circle. If you don't have something like this, people can come to your website and leave just as quickly and you'll be totally forgotten forever.

Couple of other tips with websites is to have your social media integration on them, use video as it's really powerful. You could have it pop up instantly and say hey this is who I am and why I do what I do. Pop your details in on the right hand side and I'll send you this cool resource guide instantly. It's important to have video rich websites and that they're clear and have one message. You're not everything to everyone. Have your hook around what you want to entice people with and grow it from there.

A website is an organic document, it will always grow and expand as you do, because what you know today will be different from what you know in 6–12 months' time and so on. Your website needs to grow with you.

Customer Relationship Management (CRM)

The last online aspect of communication is with the people who are now on your database. They are called customer relationship management systems and usually auto responders come with them. When someone gets that free resource guide, what happens next? Do they get a second email 2 days later? Do they get a third email another 2 days later and how are you keeping in touch with them? Are you sending out a newsletter once a month?

These are all things you need to consider, because by keeping regularly in touch with your list, but not pestering them, it will result in sales that come through maybe instantly and sometimes in 6–12 months time or longer. I've had people on my database for 2 and a half years who have come through and been converted into sales simply because I have stayed in touch and added value.

If you're brand new, start building your database today. I started with just my closest family and friends, which was about 60 or 70 people. I announced to them what I was doing and then slowly as I networked and I connected with people and I added them in, set up the website and people started putting in their details to get the freebie that I was offering. Doing more events and publicity also made my database grow into the thousands.

It's important that you are on top of that and have the basic understanding of what it is. With time automating the process and then hiring really knowledgeable experts to take care of it, you will have the best way to leverage your list. There is a famous and true saying – The Money is in the list!

As coaches, mentors or consultants we can't be great at every aspect of business. Technology is so wide and varied and it changes so fast, that once the resources are there, that is money well spent. The money that you spend with experts will gain you awesome return on investment for what you have put out there.

I want to finish of with a few words on paid advertising. It is a great avenue to generate more leads and prospects that are relevant to what you offer. This could come in the form of Google Adwords, Facebook ads or LinkedIn ads. I would be highly cautious doing it yourself because you can waste a lot of money if it's not set up properly, targeted properly and the correct pictures are not being used. When it comes to paid advertising, I would hold off until you can have an expert to help you with them, simply because I've made the mistake of doing it myself and not getting any results, wasting my time and money. Hiring someone who knows what they are doing almost guarantees you will have a fantastic return on investment.

Now is the time to put down the three things you will go and act on as a result of reading this chapter. There is a lot of stuff that I have gone over very briefly. There is an abundance of books written on online marketing. As a coach though I always say, you will be popular online when you become popular offline.

Focus on your offline activities a lot more in the early days. Keep chipping away at your online stuff by all means, because you will become better and better at it and known over a period of time. Everything will unfold organically and naturally once people know you in the offline world.

3 Actions I Commit to Taking to Create my Million Dollar Business		
		Done ✔
1		
2		
3		

Gift Resource to assist in your Development from reading this Chapter: 'Ultimate Book and Chapter Unpack Templates' as part of the Ultimate Million Dollar Coaching Business from Home Workbook available to download at: https://natasadenman.leadpages.net/milliondollarcoach/ or by scanning this QR Code with your phone.

Chapter 11
Trademark

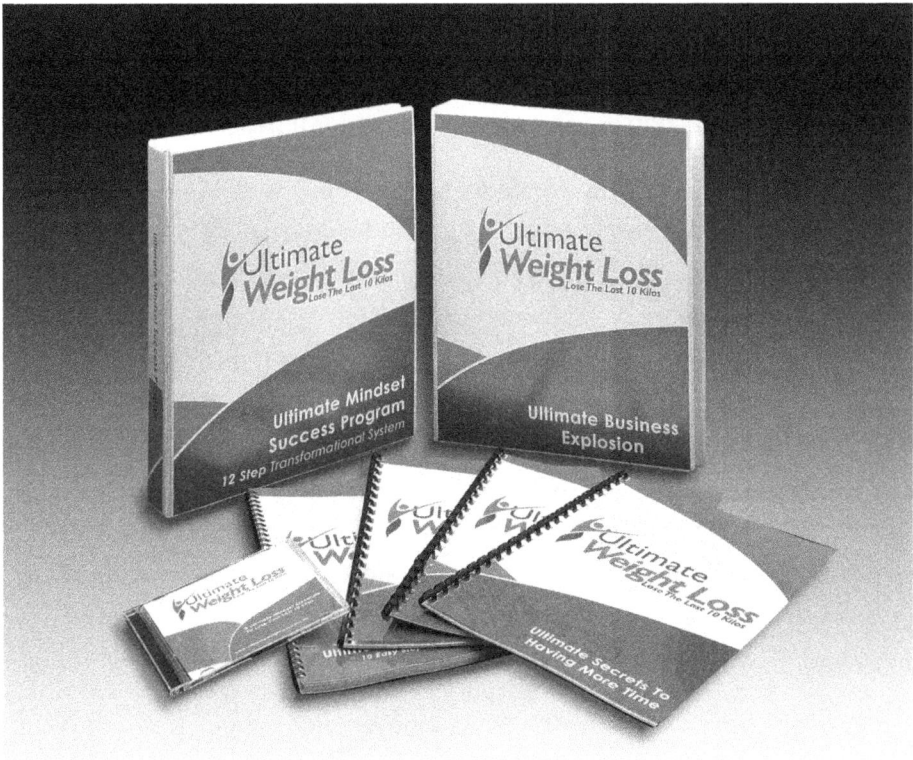

"Your smile is your logo, your personality is your business card, how you leave others feeling after an experience with you becomes your trademark."
– Jay Danzie

Trademarking is taking your business as a coach to the very next level. It comes after a period of time that you have filled your one-on-one coaching with fully booked clients. You hit that pain point where there's nothing more that you can do to generate more income for yourself or to get to the next level, which is beyond six figures then multiple six figures and eventually to your seven figure coaching practice. To get to that point, I licensed two of my brands and created intellectual property that then can be used by other people. In this chapter we're going to talk trademarking or licensing that enables you to stop selling your time for money.

It is a system that you can create that helps others who can't be bothered creating their own system to get further in their coaching businesses. You can build your wealth and your income a lot more passively and cut down the hours that you're doing one-on-one and increase your price. You would be able to work on your business a lot more, rather than in your business. You can really enter that growth and scalability stage that occurs at the point where there's a lot of demand around what you do and you're not the only person who can deliver it. It establishes your brand firmly and it adds that further credibility to what you're doing. People can see it, touch it and use it. I want to give you a few tips around how you would go about building a license system for yourself and what the important components of having it put together.

Once you have worked with clients long enough, about a year in your niche, you will start to notice patterns in how you end up helping them. These patterns are the steps that you're taking with them that can be easily documented and turned into a program that others can replicate and then buy the rights to use it. It does have some legal setup that needs to occur. People often ask me what is the difference between licensing and franchising. It is the legal structure that is more expensive to set up for franchising, which can go into hundreds of thousands of dollars where as licensing can be as little as a few thousand dollars to set up. It is a smaller version of a franchise and it's a really great way to test the waters and see if your intellectual property can be taken to that very next level where it should be franchised.

Once you notice the patterns that your clients are going through and how you have been helping them, start to document that every week. I revealed earlier in this book that with my very first book, *The 7 Ultimate Secrets to Weight Loss*, I'd sit down a couple of times twice a week to write 7 pages at a time. This would be the same to create your system. Start writing down everything that you're doing within your business. From the moment a client signs up, what kind of an email goes out? What kind of templates do you send? Do you send them a client profile? What is it that you actually do to serve them? How do you set that client up for their sessions? Do you give them tangible products or bonuses? Is there a program manual etc. etc. Start documenting all of that as you go as to document a whole business operation can be overwhelming. If you just do one little bit at a time, you sit down, put together a system and before you know it in a few months' time you will have a whole program that can then be converted into a manual. All the instructions on how someone can run your business in the way that you did to achieve the results and the success that you did.

A mistake I've seen a lot of people make is that they have created a program and a system, however they haven't added in the business growth education component. It is so important for assisting others to build the same type of business and to achieve the same type of success as the person who created that system. The reason you are reading this book is because you want to gain more business knowledge and insights around how to get your brand and your business out there so that you can finally start using your skills and talent when it comes to being a coach, a mentor or a consultant. You could be the best coach, the best mentor or the best consultant however if you don't know how to market yourself, build your credibility, share your expertise, build your community, manage your database no one's going to find out about you. Your skills will go to waste as you won't be able to end up serving those people that need your help as they won't know about you.

When becoming a coach and when people are interested in making it their career path, they fail to look into how much business support the institute/school is providing (where they are doing their training). In most cases the business side of things is not really taught at a deep enough level. You learn all the core areas required in becoming a coach, you learn all the skills but a big gap is that none provide a solid business building foundation. That is the difference that makes the difference between having hundreds of thousands of coaches in the country that are not helping many people to having a thousand coaches who are also savvy at business helping many people. If you're going to license your product or program make sure that you're also building a business growth manual to compliment it. Show them how you got to six figures. This is what I did with the Ultimate Weight Loss, Lose the Last 10 Kilos Program system. I then created a training program that was in addition to the content that was delivered in the weight loss program. That taught my licensees exactly what to do. It covered where to network, what to say, even how to run workshops. It would even teach what that call to action at the end of the workshop should be and how to convert someone from a curious prospect or a committed client. Even what sort of email you send out and what newsletter content to deliver.

When you're thinking about a licensing system, think about the two parts I mentioned. Your program is the system and the second one is how do you build the business with this particular system. You need to be savvy at both and people need to see the value in having both of those components as part of your licensed system. Where they will struggle the most is not in the delivery of your system. They will struggle with the business side that entails getting their own leads, getting prospects, getting clients. Templates, training, ongoing support, what kind of manuals will be provided and how you will price this particular program. Is it going to be a one-off cost? Are people going to re-sign every year? Are you going to keep a percentage of the sales that they have made? With the system we licensed they would re-sign as a licensee every year and they needed to purchase from us a program manual when they sign up a new client. At the end of the first year we decided to have a one-off fee where they would get access to our intellectual property for a lifetime as a way of encouraging them to continue using our system and buying manuals.

An important distinction to understand when licensing your intellectual property is that you will now be speaking to a new target market. Initially you were speaking from a business to customer target market. I was talking from my business to the person who wants to lose their last 10 kilos. Now you're moving into a place of business to business, so instead of the weight loss client I was speaking to, I needed to start marketing to the coaches, mentors, health and wellness practitioners who would be interested in delivering my ultimate mindset success system. Now these people had different frustrations to my original avatar for my weight loss program. The frustrations of having those extra 10 kilos for the client are different to the frustrations of a business owner. They perhaps can't get their clients to lose weight or achieve a strong mindset around their health so for them it was about bringing in a program to their clientele so they would achieve great results in their expertise. The advice that they were giving through their other skills, this was added to with my secondary mindset program that they could deliver to achieve a higher percentage of results and have people succeeding on their particular programs.

You need to have two separate websites for your two offerings. One website can't talk to two different target markets, as they have different pain points, different frustrations and different outcomes that they're looking for. We tried to keep everything on one website in the beginning of our journey into licensing, but there was a point when we just needed to bite the bullet and set up a second website. That's why now that I'm running 5 brands I've got 5 websites, because they're all talking to a different ideal client. If you want to see the difference in the websites go to visit ultimateweightloss.com.au then visit ultimateweightlossbusiness. com and you'll see how one talks to the weight loss client and the other one talks to the business owner who's working in the health and wellness industry.

There is so much that you need to think about, prepare and pull together so that you will be able to sell the licensing over and over. These days we don't focus as much on selling our weight loss licensing. We actually ended up licensing our Ultimate Business Edge brand so that people have the opportunity to be business coaches. They can now help other businesses packaging services, and building products of profit so we've got those two different businesses in a box. All of our licensees have a full system delivering everything step-by-step to their clients.

It is not necessary that you just focus on that one thing all of the time. We have gone on this entrepreneurial journey and as you grow and evolve, you may think of other ideas. The ideas you had before are not wasted as your intellectual property can be used in many different ways. Nothing you do in your business is going to be a waste. You can end up selling it and you can sell a particular brand down the line, as long as this is properly structured and streamlined. You can give things away as lead generation resources because intellectual property doesn't expire. Can you re-label it? Can you put a different name on it? Can you re-launch it out there to another market? There is always ways to use and repurpose you intellectual property.

A challenge that may arise on this journey into licensing is that some of your licensees may not get the results that you intended them to get. As long as you make sure that you bring in the value and that you're offering the support, if they're not getting the results, it's not your responsibility. There's a saying, you can take a horse to water, but you can't make him drink. Just make sure that you are doing what you have promised, that you're delivering the value and you're updating your systems regularly. From the beginning, you're not going to get everything 100% right and remember, nothing is ever going to be 100% right. It might be right for 5 minutes or a few days or even weeks, however you'll evolve and realise that this template would be better for them to use. You will know you haven't taught them this particular method because you yourself just discovered it. Now and then add in an extra support call or webinar, however you plan to do it so you can communicate and add value to your licensees. Make sure that you are constantly evolving and growing and keeping in touch with your people.

If they're not being responsive it's okay because everyone has their own lives. Their priorities might change and sometimes the focus may not be there like it was when they signed on as a licensee. It might have been at a certain point in time, but now it isn't. Just think how you will approach this, as your mindset in being a licensor will be challenged as well. You will think, I used this system and I did it for myself and I know it works so why aren't people getting results? Are they following the steps? So long as you are mentoring them, as that's what your role is, your role isn't to go get their clients and create their own businesses for them because every single person is responsible for their own success. When you take that on board and you just realise that the people that you work with will be a lot easier to deal with, as they have to come from a place of understanding. You need to educate them on this. Let them know, I'm here to help you. However, at the end of the day you have to go out there and push yourself out of your comfort zone, talk to people, create your workshops and generate your leads and learn how to develop some of the technical aspect of your business.

Always make sure you offer help. Be open and even offer unlimited support for your licensees. Let them know that they can phone you up. Trust me, people are not going to overwhelm you. There will be some people who are high maintenance and others who are lower maintenance so it all balances out. The beauty is that you're open to giving that support and that's the important thing, the intention needs to be there. If they do ring you, be responsive; be quick to get back to them, because it's the experience of working with you that you're selling. It is not so much what or how you're delivering, it's more what experience they are getting if they're working through your licensing system.

You just need to think, is this licensing another thing you would take on in your business? Nothing is wasted if you do go through the process and it doesn't work. You can always use those systems in other ways and share them to further help your clients.

Now, write down the three things you are going to complete as a result of reading this chapter. Also, write down the ideas you have for the future. This doesn't happen overnight or even should be a focus for the next 12 moths. If you're just starting out you can't action this step until later down the track as you need to have the success that your potential licensees will want to learn from.

3 Actions I Commit to Taking to Create my Million Dollar Business		
		Done ✔
1		
2		
3		

Gift Resource to assist in your Development from reading this Chapter: 'Ultimate Book and Chapter Unpack Templates' as part of the Ultimate Million Dollar Coaching Business from Home Workbook available to download at: https://natasadenman.leadpages.net/milliondollarcoach/ or by scanning this QR Code with your phone.

Chapter 12
Attitude

"Success is often achieved by those who don't know that failure is inevitable."
– Coco Chanel

Your altitude in life is determined by your attitude. To get to a certain level of success, you need to have the mindset skills to overcome the mental funk that can arise so frequently early on in your journey. This is the last chapter of this book, however, it's something that must be used in every single area of the journey of building a business. Being successful at things that you want to be successful at, whether it's with your family, your relationships, your health and ultimately building that seven figure coaching business. When you have the mindset skills and a toolbox to access in those tough situations, you will be able to overcome those setbacks that happen early on in business.

Mindset also builds character, strength, confidence, persistence and it gives you that ability to keep going, while others quit. Trust me, a lot of people quit. If it were easy, everyone would be doing it. By achieving that new strong mindset, this is your key and entry to the new world and the life of your dreams. So what is attitude? Well according to Google, it's a predisposition or a tendency to respond positively or negatively towards a certain idea, object, person, or situation. Attitude influences an individual's choice of action, and responses for challenges incentives and rewards. As human beings we are more driven to avoid pain than to experience pleasure. This is where the real challenge lies. Human beings tend to focus more on that instant pain, or instant reward that they can get, rather than the delayed pain and the delayed reward.

Let's look at an example. Instant pain is getting up in front of a group of people and speaking at that networking event. Instant pleasure is staying behind your computer, comfortable at home and not having to face anyone. Would that get you to business success? I doubt it. Delayed pain is not being able to pay your bills, not being able to continue running your business and going back to a job. Delayed pleasure is where you have achieved your ultimate lifestyle and you're living the life of your dreams on *your* terms. Unfortunately most people give into that instant pain or pleasure and fail to focus on the delayed pain or pleasure. My number one tip for you, and this actually applies in different areas of your life as well such as your health, your relationships, and you communication; it is always much better to do the things that will ultimately get us to the results that we want no matter how uncomfortable they make us feel.

In this final chapter I want to share with you my top 7-mindset strategies that have got me to where I am today. There's more than 7, however the brain loves 7's, so I will share with you what I do on a daily basis to be able to keep myself fresh, motivated and inspired. This is how I am able to handle those moments, where I am rejected and I'm feeling like things are going backwards. In business we are going to go two steps forward and one backwards, sometimes two steps back and then we must keep going forward.

My number 1 attitude adjuster is:

Schedule for success

Tony Robbins has the saying, what gets scheduled gets done. This is so true and this is why I use a physical diary where I can physically write down my appointments. I have a separate to-do list where I cluster the smaller tasks that I want to complete. That way I come back to it when I am free and do it in clustered time blocks. Whenever I have written down something, even if I don't end up looking back at it, it gets done. It's as if it's been engraved in the back of my mind as to what my intention was. Through the sheer writing down of the information that you want to execute, you are actually putting the intention out there that you will do it. My diary is full of little ticks and hardly any crosses, because whenever I want to achieve something, I schedule it in. That's my commitment to myself that I will make it happen. You know the saying, *don't fail to plan because you will plan to fail*.

My number 2 attitude adjuster is:

Act before you feel

At times we give into our negative feelings of emotions and fear that is not real. We don't want to get up in the morning to do that exercise. We don't want to come out of the house to go to that networking event because we're fearful that we may not belong or that it's going to be hard and tiring. If we just shut that down, that part of us down and just took the action without thinking too much, you will have much better feelings at the other end. It's like the saying, 'Say yes, than work out the how'. Sometimes you just don't know exactly how the how will come, but by backing yourself and saying yes, the universe aligns and gives you the tools and the resources that you need. The universe can see that you have had the courage to stand up and actually say yes to the opportunity that you have in front of you.

My number 3 attitude adjuster is:

Invest in shortcuts

We spoke all the way back in the first part of this section of the book about shortcuts and having a mentor and that has been an integral part of the success I've been able to achieve. Modelling excellence, people who have achieved results you're after, hanging out with them and asking lots of questions. Being curious about what they did, how did they do it, how did they think in situations where they've had setbacks, and what are some strategies that you can replicate for yourself to achieve that same result in a much shorter time. Thinking about your investments as an investment, not a cost, because those short cuts have occurred or have been created because someone has made a lot of mistakes on our behalf. It is very important to look at that and appreciate that about people who have that excellence that you're looking for as they are the ones that have made the mistakes so you can avoid them.

My number 4 attitude adjuster is:

Get comfortable with being uncomfortable

This might sound really scary, however the more uncomfortable you are on your journey of building your business the better it is and the more familiar it becomes. As much as it's scary and you are filled with fear and reservation on taking action on certain things, I can guarantee you that I now thrive on being uncomfortable, because I know it means I'll learn something new and I'll be able to step up to the very next level of achieving the goals I want to achieve. Familiarity with being uncomfortable comes as you do that thing more often and the more you do something, the more you become a master at it. They say, *repetition is the mother of all skill*. If you repeat being uncomfortable many times over, you'll become more skillful at being uncomfortable therefore keep stretching and growing in your business.

My number 5 attitude adjuster is:

Forget about the competition; focus on being the best you can possibly be

Some people will do it better, worse, about the same, who cares? Focus on your world; focus on how you can bring out and serve people the best way that you can. On my journey I have not done much research on who is doing what, what's popular out there, what's ranking better or the trends. I just looked at myself and discovered the gold within me and know that I will attract the right people. I'm not saying that's the right way to do it, it's just my way. That's been the thing that's enabled me to really be in line with what I'm delivering and attracted people to me. They want to access that same part of themselves of what they stand for and what that provides. As a coach especially, people buy people and they want something that's really within you, not so much out there in the marketplace, because you're unique. There's only one of you in this world. The day that you realise how special you are, that you're the only one that can provide the experience, the system, the way that you say it, the way that you do it is the day you will start to flourish. Just like you see a lot of very successful people have their own personal flavour, so do you. You have that flavour within you, so use it to your advantage and be proud to have that because no one else can replicate that. That's what makes you special and unique and makes you so significant in this world. That's an awesome belief to take on board, then that is actually what you will start seeing being projected back into your world.

My number 6 attitude adjuster is:

Double your rate of failure

There have been thousands of quotes about how failure is an essential ingredient to success. Nine out of 10 things you try will generally not work, especially when it comes to marketing. By doubling your rate of failure you will actually get closer to success, because you will eliminate things that are not working for you and get to a point where you will have the results that you want. Success is not luck. It is about taking those logical steps to get to where you're going and along the journey of those logical steps you will certainly make mistakes. You are a unique person who will find their own journey, their own recipe and how you can make that happen for yourself.

My number 7 attitude adjuster is:

Celebrate and reward yourself

Celebrate your wins. Don't just focus on the moments where you feel like you're hitting rock bottom. Talk to people and be proud to share your successes. It will be a balancing act between successes and setbacks and failures and things that you achieve that you never thought possible. Make sure you make them really big as the highs in business are really high and the lows can be so very low. It's not a very steady line like when you were an employee. I always say, as an employee you don't need faith. As a business owner you must have faith, as sometimes it will feel like you're losing your whole business overnight. There are other times when business is in a real lull for you yet other times it will seem like this business is going to triple in the next three months or three years with spectacular growth. Reward yourself early on. I used to set myself little $20–$30 rewards, every time I would sign up a client, and when I would do that I'd feel really deserving to walk into the store and buy what I had chosen for my reward. As time progresses I started rewarding my children and sharing my successes with them and enjoying the fruits of my labour. What's the point of stacking up money in a bank account where you don't enjoy the lifestyle you're creating with that business?

I'm smart about our investments and I always put money away yet at the same time you can have that cash flow where you can enjoy the little pleasures that come every day in your life. It's a reward in itself to not have to think about buying a cup of coffee as can happen early on in the journey. You think about every dollar that goes towards just little every day expenses. I love the fact that now we can just go and spend a few hundred dollars and enjoy an afternoon or a morning of whatever we feel like doing.

What happens if you are hitting those roadblocks and you can't seem to move through them? I would ask, are you still trying to do it all alone? Get someone external to review your strategy and business model and advise you what your next steps are. Find a few people that you can speak to and be heard from and decide to be part of a bigger community and a tribe that is going on the same journey that you are. If you take a long time to get through mindset issues and that mental funk occurs, some of the things I have found really helpful over the last few years is to start reading books that will inspire me and motivate me. I also listen to audio books in the car while I'm driving. Little short YouTube videos can be great. I'll go on YouTube and I'll search for something and I just trust that the right message will come through that particular video I get shown. You don't need to spend hours on your personal development every day, it might just be a 10-minute boost that you need.

Practising gratitude is really great before you wake up for the day. What are the things that you're grateful for? It doesn't have to be the big things, you can choose little things that make you smile. Those are the things I do when going through a phase where I feel disconnected with myself and am having a lot of mindset setbacks and I feel like I can't break through. If you know that you're on your own and you just can't get out of your despair, acknowledge this and what you're doing as a first step. Be aware that's what's happening to you then revisit the 7 attitude adjusters and take action on them. Start doing something different. We know the definition of insanity is doing the same thing over and over and expecting a different result. Do something different to create a different result and a different outcome and surround yourself by people who will support you. They can lift you up and give you the ability to show that best version of you and surround yourself with those people that lift you higher and don't drag you down.

Now it's your turn. What are three things that you will do as a result of reading this chapter? Perhaps you'll choose your top three attitude adjusters, or something that you will act on when that mindset funk starts to creep in. Go ahead now, fill out your table and I trust that this has been a valuable and insightful journey for you.

3 Actions I Commit to Taking to Create my Million Dollar Business		
		Done ✔
1		
2		
3		

Gift Resource to assist in your Development from reading this Chapter: 'Ultimate Book and Chapter Unpack Templates' as part of the Ultimate Million Dollar Coaching Business from Home Workbook available to download at: https://natasadenman.leadpages.net/milliondollarcoach/ or by scanning this QR Code with your phone.

Afterword

Growing up surrounded by four very strong women, I worked out that there was a core 'why' that was driving me to achieve the success that I did. I had built this belief as a young girl: that men can't financially look after women. Because of the insecurity that I felt growing up not being supported by my father and some of the mistakes and other male role models I have had in my life to prove to me that this belief was true. When we believe something to be true, we keep seeking out evidence to prove to ourselves that it is. That evidence keeps popping up no matter how much we don't want it to.

It's interesting how our why is actually deep down engrained from our past and our imprint period. I would love for you to explore that for yourself now that you have arrived at this part of the book and you have this desire to succeed and build a million dollar coaching business from home. Find your 'why' and decide that there is no option, because if you want success as badly as you must breathe, then you will get there no matter what.

Some people get there sooner, some people get there later, so long as you're taking the steps that are required to get to your success, then you will get there without a doubt. Another thing is I want you to consider the difference between you walking around saying I want a successful business, I choose to have a successful business, or I commit to having a successful business. There's a very big difference between those three sentences of wanting, choosing and committing.

The first one starts off from a very childish attitude, where a lot of people walk around saying, I want a successful business, I want to lose weight, I want to have a wonderful relationship, yet they're not willing to do whatever it takes to get there.

When you say I choose, that means that you are conscious of taking responsibility and having choice, whether you will or will not have a successful business. The commitment is the most responsible and adult-like behaviour. When you think of commitment, think of a wedding. At a wedding, when you commit to your partner, husband or wife, what happens at the first fight or disagreement that you have? You don't just leave that marriage. You've committed to each other for life and you work out other ways to get through your problems and challenges.

That is the same approach I would love for you to take with your business. You don't quit every time there's a lull, a setback, a no, you're feeling rejected or you're feeling like you don't belong. You don't quit, you keep going, because as you become better at it, it will swing the other way.

So start taking those steps. Be flexible and open to learn new skills along the way. Be flexible also to change what isn't working. Bring consistency into your every day routine when it comes to your business, because consistency is king.

Have a commitment to completion. Every successful person completes their projects from start to finish. There's an old saying, that if you help others get their dreams, your dreams will be taken care of. Focus on serving and giving freely to people, because you will get it back. The law of reciprocity says that you will get it in return and sometimes tenfold.

Make sure your business is created around your highest values. This year alone I've come to an insight, that one of my highest values is to run my business fast and fun. So if things are not fun and they're not able to be executed quickly, then I don't have too much interest in pursuing them. Understand where your values are and how that is supporting you in achieving the success that you want.

I've said it before and I'll say it again – Get a Mentor. Invest in those short cuts, courses, educational platforms that will save you time and money and heartache in the long run. They are the ones that will show you the right steps to take so that you get to your goals in the shortest time possible. Look to model those that are ahead of you and that you admire.

Commit to celebrating and rewarding yourself. Commit to constant and never-ending improvement that as human beings we are driven by. Most importantly, back yourself, work on your confidence and certainty, which comes from action and be the person you want to be, because it will come through in the actions that you take.

Now that you have collected a wealth of information, it's time to turn that information into knowledge. Knowledge is only attained through experience. All of those things that you committed to do in each of the chapters, you need to now go back and start ticking off and putting them into action. Once you have put them into action, the information you have learnt will slowly start to transition into knowledge that you will have. When you're doing it, you know it. When you're not doing it, you don't know it.

About the Author

Natasa Denman was born and raised in Skopje, Macedonia up to the age 14 after which she immigrated to Melbourne Australia with her mum. She didn't speak English and found it challenging in the first two years to fit into the new country and culture. Her zest for learning and achievement fast tracked this process and she had high performance results in her academic endeavours.

Natasa has a Bachelor of Applied Science (Psychology/Psychophysiology), Diploma in Life Coaching, NLP Practitioner Certification, and Practitioner of Matrix Therapies, holds a Black Belt in Taekwondo and is a Professional Certified Coach (PCC) through the International Coaching Federation.

Being creative and writing books is something she never planned to do. Her passion for business and marketing was the reason she wrote her first

book *The 7 Ultimate Secrets to Weight Loss* in June 2011. This book put her first business on the map and enabled her husband to join her full time in the business a year later. She is also a contributor of *You Can … Live the Life of Your Dreams, a co-author of Ninja Couch Marketing and author of Ultimate 48 Hour Author*.

Ultimate 48 Hour Author came about as a result of the success books have brought to Natasa's 4 businesses. Aside from books she has also written 5 programs and has 3 Licensed systems that are being used by others internationally in their businesses.

Natasa is a mum of three, Judd (6), Mika (3) and Xara (3 Months). She loves living her Ultimate Lifestyle. Natasa nowadays mentors and coaches: consultants, speakers, entrepreneurs and small business owners to become published authors and become the authority leaders in their fields. With her Brilliant Ultimate 48-Hour Author Blueprint enabling busy professionals to get their book completed within just 48 hours, her program is highly sought after by those who are looking to influence their market and explode their credibility and standing.

As a highly skilled business mentor and coach, Natasa knows that writing your book is only just the beginning and uses her marketing and publicity knowledge to make sure that all of her authors get the results they are looking for with a strategic business plan which outlines the step-by-step process that needs to be followed. With 100% success rate from all attendees at her retreats, The Ultimate 48-Hour Blueprint is the first choice for business owners looking for the competitive edge.

Natasa's Websites:

www.natasadenman.com

www.ultimate48hourauthor.com.au

Email: natasa@natasadenman.com

Work with Natasa

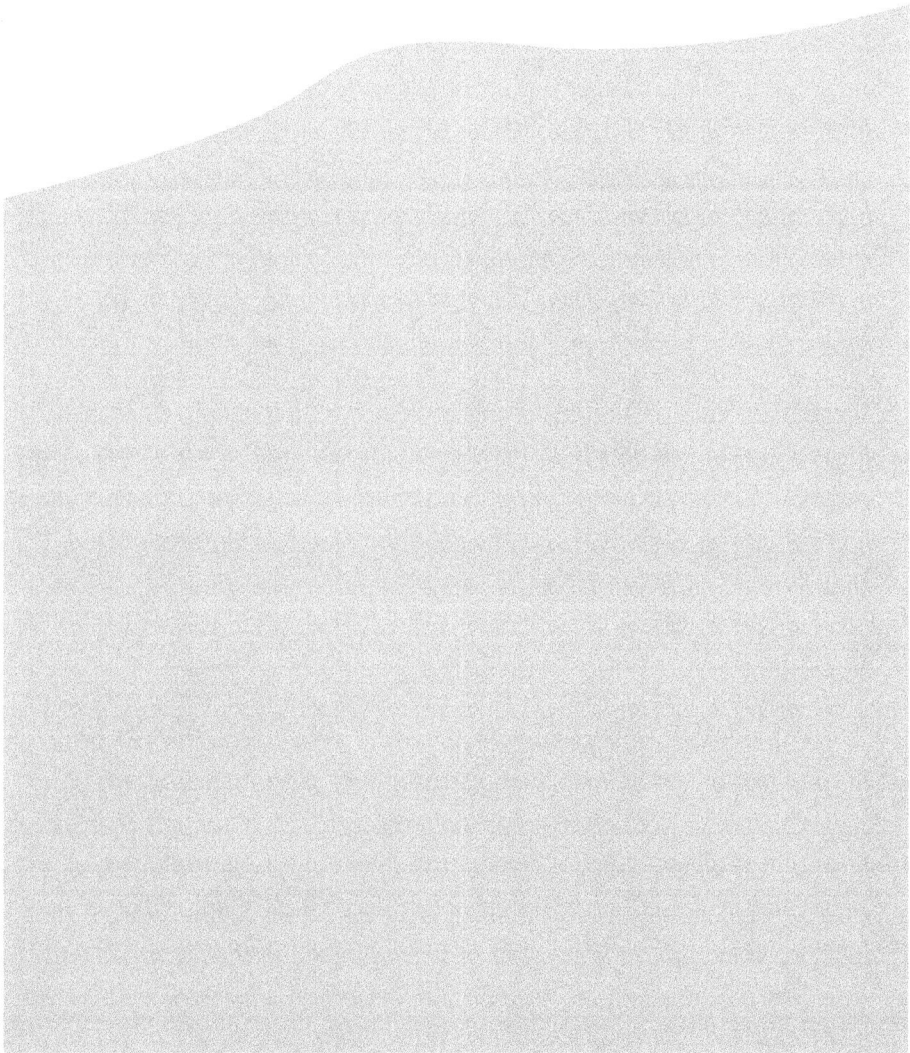

"Working with Natasa as a member of her inner circle mentor program, I have learnt so much and implemented many changes to increase my business and allow it to grow. Natasa is free-giving of her information and answers any questions without a second thought. Natasa is the nicest person I have ever met and welcomes anyone to her circle, virtually and in person."

– Emily Obouhoff
Company Accountant at DCE
(Inner Circle Member of Ultimate Business Edge)

"Before joining the Ultimate Mastermind Mentoring Program, I was not getting far in my business at all. I knew I had a lot to learn and having been mentored by Natasa before, this program seemed the logical choice to join. After the very first call, I was instantly inspired to do even more in my business. It has a great structure, a leader who is the ultimate role model mum in business and massive support provided.

"I was given tools to improve my cash flow from the get go, so I could focus on other business building activities as we went along. The content that has been shared right throughout has been excellent and very cutting edge. Each and every webinar builds on the previous and allows for challenges in our personal businesses to be put in the spotlight so it can be assessed and the power of the mastermind steps in to help overcome and triumph.

"The accountability is very powerful as being an entrepreneur working from home can be a lonely journey so the support from the other business owners in the group has been powerful. Another part that has been outstanding is being given knowledge on business and mindset challenges that come up in stages of business. To be in a position to see what's coming up in the stage of business I'm at and then to be able to make the best decision to continue on through any challenge without the heartache, has been one of the best parts of the program.

"The small numbers in the group means there is personal attention given in the program. I can't thank Natasa enough for what she has done in this program and I can't recommend this program enough. It truly is a powerful way to grow your business and being partnered in success."

– Grace Vassallo
Behind The Hair (Ultimate Mastermind Mentoring Program)

"Natasa Denman is just amazing – as a successful entrepreneur, mentor, friend and human being. It has been a privilege having Natasa as my mentor. Her mentoring approach is full of care and support, and also some tough love when needed. Working with her has been such a fun and memorable experience. Natasa is someone who walks her talk (she only teaches what she has done and tested), holds you accountable on your journey and most important of all, believes in you and your potential (especially at times when you have doubt in yourself).

"This year I had the privilege to be a part of Natasa's Ultimate 48 Hour Author Weekend and have now become a proud author of my book: 'Honeymoon Forever – Love & Passion That Lasts A Lifetime'. I wouldn't have done it without her! I am now a part of her Ultimate Mastermind Mentoring Program where I continue to be mentored by Natasa, and be supported by another eleven amazing entrepreneurs. What a great community to be a part of!

"Natasa is someone I truly admire as a mentor and adore as a friend. She is honest, fun, action-packed and very caring. I am so grateful to have met such an amazing woman like Natasa and feel truly honored to be mentored by someone who has achieved great amazing success. Thank you Natasa for everything you have done for me!"

– Jane Nguyen
Author, Speaker and Relationship Expert of 'Honeymoon Forever'
(Ultimate 48 Hour Author Retreat Attendee Feb 2013, One on One Mentoring Client and Member of the Ultimate Mastermind Mentoring Program)

The Being Comes with the Doing!

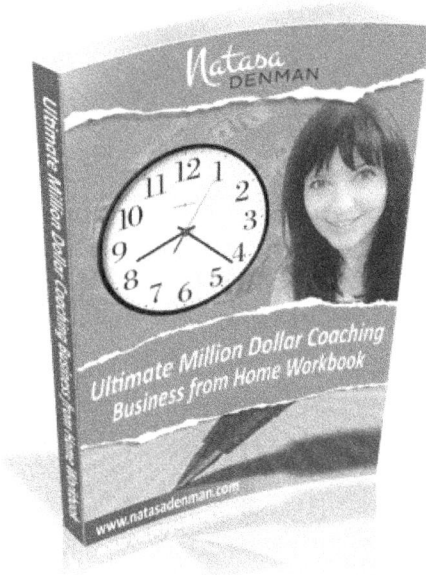

Download your FREE Ultimate Million Dollar Coaching Business from Home Workbook NOW to start turning the Information into Knowledge. Over 30 pages of Templates and Samples that will propel you to greater clarity, direction and action with your business. By getting this Workbook you will also become a part of our Ultimate Community where you will be invited to join VIP trainings and gain access to free resources along the way.

Your Workbook is available instantly via this link:
https://natasadenman.leadpages.net/millondollarcoach

Natasa DENMAN

Due Out Feb 2015

Natasa Denman is The Ultimate 48-Hour Author. After publishing her fourth book early in 2014, she now mentors and coaches speakers, entrepreneurs and business owners to become published authors and become the authority leaders in their fields. With her Brilliant Ultimate 48-Hour Author Blueprint enabling busy professionals to get their book completed within just 48 hours, her program is highly sought after by those who are looking to influence their market and explode their credibility and standing.

As a highly skilled business mentor and coach, Natasa knows that writing your book is only just the beginning and utilises her marketing and publicity knowledge to make sure that all of her authors get the results they are looking for with a strategic business plan which outlines the step-by-step process that needs to be followed. With 100% success rate from all attendees at her retreats, The Ultimate 48-Hour Blueprint is the first choice for business owners looking for the competitive edge.

Natasa is a sought after speaker on the following topics:

Author Your Way to Business Success
- How to position a book lucratively for your Brand
- Building Leverage with your book
- The secret to writing your book in just 48 hours

Mumpreneur Secrets to a Profitable Business from Home
- Juggling Babies and business with success
- Replacing selling your time for money for profit
- Finding Flow and Time for Your Ultimate Lifestyle

Ultimate Expert Positioning Formula
- The 3 Keys to positioning as an expert
- One reason why people fail to establish themselves as the expert
- Leveraging your Expert Status for profit

Contact Info: 0412 085 160
www.natasadenman.com
natasa@natasadenman.com

Ultimate Mastermind

- **Are you struggling to get clients?**
- **Do you seem to be working hard for little results?**
- **Do you feel super busy and chasing your tail?**
- **Are you uncertain of what your next steps are to a profitable business?**
- **Are you ready to do something about your CHALLENGE NOW?**

Why would you join?
- Fast results for your small business
- The Power of the Mastermind to propel you to success
- Huge accountability and follow up structure
- Weekly Strategy sessions to keep you progressing rapidly
- Mentorship by a million dollar business owner

What does it include?
- Fortnightly online meetings (max 12 members on the call) with Natasa Denman
- Alternate fortnightly check in calls with your Power Team (4-6 max per Team)
- Access to a Huge Library of Pre-recorded business growth trainings and webinars
- Unlimited E-Mail Support
- Membership to the Inner Circle which has an additional 90 Minute support call per month

How do I qualify?
- 100% Commitment to your business growth
- Willingness to follow through on strategies and tasks
- Contribution to the others in the group and team and encouragement towards everyone's success
- Leave your excuses behind
- Commit to this process for a minimum of 3, 6 or 12 months to get optimum results (Pricing structure with Bonuses discussed over a 20 minute qualifying conversation)
- Be willing to financially invest in yourself to make this work

Mentoring Program

What if...

- I can't make some of the schedule times? All core Mastermind mentoring calls will be recorded and available to listen to at your convenience. We encourage you do your best to come live for maximum value and experience of the program.
- I find my business needs more personal attention? One on one mentoring is available as an option with rates starting at $3000 per month depending on the business and needs.

Over 6 Months you will get insights and mentoring around the following topics:

1. Ultimate Mindset Success to Riches
2. Clarifying your Message and Unique Value Proposition
3. Structuring Your Offerings for maximum Leverage
4. Ultimate Marketing Madness to Maximise Lead Generation
5. Offline Strategies to get Your Clients Fast
6. Running and Filling Workshops for Profit
7. Sales Conversion Tools and the Psychology behind it
8. Establishing Value and Overcoming Objections in Selling
9. Working Smarter not Harder for Profit
10. How to create an arsenal of Intellectual Property
11. Publicity Secrets for Free Media Exposure
12. Your Ultimate Lifestyle

Are You Ready to Get Serious About Your Business?

By application Only – Email: natasa@natasadenman.com

Ultimate 48 Hour Author Retreats

Does this sound like you? Are you still …

- **Thinking of writing that book but unsure how to get started,**

- **Sick of sharing your gifts & brilliant insight without receiving sufficient income,**

- **Struggling to get exposure and be an Authority in your Niche,**

- **Unsure how to shift from where you are to where you want to be,**

- **Confused on how to package and position yourself as an expert and raise your fees,**

- **Lacking the visibility needed to stand out, attract your ideal clients effortlessly, and elevate your influence significantly,**

- **Tired of being the best kept secret in your industry or in the marketplace,**

- **Feeling stagnant with regard to growing your business, profits, and profile,**

- **Lacking guidance from an experienced mentor and book authority who is ready and able to hold your hand, listen to your heart & dreams, and then take you exactly where you want to go,**

Becoming an author is the Easiest and most Powerful Strategy to accelerate your Influence, set you up as an Authority and influence the Masses!

Visibility changes everything. Ultimately, we both know that if more people knew about you, could read about you and see you, you'd be able to change more lives and increase your income dramatically. And, if you had more training, you could really captivate your audience not only with your written words but from the stage.

Natasa Denman runs 4 Ultimate 48 Hour Author Retreats each Year

All her attendees are now published authors achieving amazing success in their Businesses.

More Information at www.ultimate48hourauthor.com.au

Ultimate 48 Hour Author Retreats	Silver	Gold	Platinum
Mentoring & Accountability			
2 Hour Pre Weekend Prep Session One on One	✔	✔	✔
Unlimited Email Support	✔	✔	✔
Laser Mentoring until Book Release	✔	✔	✔
Ultimate 48 Hour Author Weekend Training & Support Including:	✔	✔	✔
1. Speaking Success System	✔	✔	✔
2. The Power of Social Media	✔	✔	✔
3. Connecting Through Video	✔	✔	✔
4. Free Publicity Generation	✔	✔	✔
5. Successful Publicity Follow Up System	✔	✔	✔
6. Pre-Launch Campaign	✔	✔	✔
7. Your Mindset Success	✔	✔	✔
Essentials for Success	✔	✔	✔
Luxury Accomodation	✔	✔	✔
Restaurant Style Meals	✔	✔	✔
Transcription of Your Book - 7 Hours Max		✔	✔
Webinar Set Up and Promotion to Explode Your Book Sales		✔	✔
Essential Checklist to Prepare You for the Weekend		✔	✔
Checklists/Guides up to Publishing Handover		✔	✔
Pre-Launch Campaign Set Up		✔	✔
Publishing		✔	✔
ISBN/Barcode		✔	✔
Copyeditting (40 000 words max)		✔	✔
Internal Layout		✔	✔
Cover Creation (Including 3D Version)		✔	✔
100 Books (Black and White internal printing)		✔	✔
Author Photoshoot		✔	✔
E-Book Version of the Book		✔	✔
Library Deposit		✔	✔
Bonuses		✔	✔
Ultimate Product Generator Manual and Training Footage		✔	✔
Ninja Couch Marketing & Ultimate 48 Hour Author Books		✔	✔
Social Media Made Easy		✔	✔
Secrets to Running Webinars for Profit		✔	✔
12 Ninja Stars to Business Explosion E-Course (10 Hrs)		✔	✔
10 Easy Steps to Bust Your Money Limiting Beliefs		✔	✔
Ultimate Busines Support Inner Circle Membership Lifetime		✔	✔
One on One Mentoring Support (3 Months)			✔

By Application Only email: book@ultimate48hourauthor.com.au